I Will Fear No Evil

by Vlado Fajfr
as told to
Ruth Stewart Fajfr
and
Sheila Stewart Doom

Revival Literature
P.O. Box 6068 • Asheville, NC 28816
USA

ISBN 1-56632-096-8

Copyright © 1995 by Revival Literature. All rights reserved. No reproduction in any form of this book, in whole or in part, except for brief quotations in articles or reviews, may be made without written permission from Revival Literature, P. O. Box 6068, Asheville, NC 28816.

Printed in the United States of America.

Foreword

I Will Fear No Evil is more than a biography of an unusual servant of God. It is a heart-warming story of hope and encouragement for that Christian who longs to live for the glory of his Master.

In this brief look into the life and ministry of Dr. Vlado Fajfr, you will witness a man living for Christ in a hostile environment. As a young man newly born into the family of God, Vlado stands valiantly against the pressure of his peers luring him back into the world. When Hitler's Nazi invaders storm across Czechoslovakia, Vlado continues to spread the Gospel "in villages, in hospitals, in prisons, on trains, and in the open air." Even in the midst of the iron rule of Communism gripping Czechoslovakia following World War II, this persevering saint of God presses on fearlessly in service for the Lord.

Locked in a prison cell. Confined to a hospital bed. Beaten cruelly in a KGB interrogation room. Standing by the cold graveside of a departed loved one. Vlado Fajfr never loses sight of the Lord Who works all things together "for the good of them that love God."

As one has said before, the man who fears God need fear nothing else. This book reveals such a man.

If in your walk with the Lord you are facing overwhelming difficulties and heartaches, *I Will Fear No Evil* will stir your soul to look beyond the battles to the One Who reigns— the Lord God Omnipotent.

— Charles L. Alligood

Contents

Prologue 7
What kind of joy comes out of a bottle? 9
Lord, I believe! 15
Vlado Fajfr, you have become a fool! 21
We were glad to hear your words of God's love 25
Vlado finds a bride 31
I got it from the Lord 35
He who risks nothing, gains nothing 41
We are witnesses of the power of the Holy Ghost 45
Watch, stand firm, be courageous 51
What does this mean, Lord? 55
Oh, Lord, set me free! 59
Lord, I thank you 65
All things work together for good 73
A witness wherever he goes 83
You no longer have permission to preach 91
The Lord takes Jirina home 99
You are the Lord's choice for me! 103
To all the nations 107
The wind bloweth where it listeth 111
It might be good for me to leave Usti 117
Foreigners are invading our fair city 121
Epilogue 125

•••

Photographs .... Special Center Section

Prologue
Banska Bystrica: 1950

The blows to my head have left me confused though still conscious. Feeling my face swelling, I touch my nose gingerly and look down. Blood is on my hand. As I shake my head to clear it, I still hear men shouting at me, taunting me, accusing me.

But now—now it is over.

> Thank you, dear Father. I did not dishonor Your Name.

Slowly, my mind drifts to another place, to another beating. Two men are in a filthy Philippian jail, backs bleeding, feet in stocks, but singing, yes, singing.

> Ho, my comrades! see the signal Waving in the sky!
> Reinforcements now appearing, Victory is nigh!
> See the mighty host advancing, Satan leading on,
> Mighty men around us falling, Courage almost gone!

I am surprised at the strength of my voice.

> Hold the fort for I am coming, Jesus signals still. . . .

A loud banging on the door of my cell suddenly interrupts:

> Stop your singing. You're disturbing the other prisoners.

1
What kind of joy comes out of a bottle?
Chleb: 1936

The twenty or so university students making their way to the ski lodge on top of Mt. Chleb were in a cheerful mood. Fresh snow had fallen across the Fatra Mountains and the slopes glistened in the brilliance of an unusually fine Slovakian day. Even the sun appeared to be cooperating with the dreams of these future lawyers, doctors, philosophers, and engineers—dreams of a two week holiday filled with skiing, dancing, and drinking.

The students, nearly all of whom were members of Brno's climbing club, were making the most of their post-Christmas vacation, skiing in the mornings, and basking in the warm sun in the afternoons. Each night they reveled in the music, dancing, drinking, and usual pleasures of young people with plenty of time and money.

As December 30, 1936, began, there was nothing to suggest that the day would be different from any other. At least not until one of the students discovered that his ski strap was loose. Sliding to a stop, Vlado Fajfr stooped to adjust his strap. When he looked up, he saw that the others had left him behind.

"It doesn't matter," the young law student thought to himself. "I'll take a short cut and reach the bottom about the same time they do."

The snow under Vlado's feet was perfect for skiing. Besides, he was a good skier, known for his confidence and daring on the slopes. He ignored the fresh snow which had begun to fall, causing poor visibility.

With breathtaking speed he glided down the steep slope in pursuit of his friends. Suddenly he began to skid and, losing his balance, fell headlong in the snow.

"Impossible!" Vlado muttered to himself angrily, but nevertheless glad none of his friends were around to witness his *stupid* fall. "I have skied every day this week without falling. Why in the world should I do it now?"

At that moment Vlado looked down the path ahead of him. A number of huge rocks, which he had not noticed before because of the falling snow, lay in his path. Surely he would have been killed instantly, or crippled for life had he continued as he had been going!

Shocked and sobered at the very thought of what might have happened, Vlado whispered half aloud, "Mother's prayers! God has intervened to save my life in answer to Mother's prayers."

* * *

Vlado Fajfr was the son of Christian parents. His father was a bank manager who also served as a lay preacher. Mr. Fajfr had founded two local churches in Moravia, and now he was a very active member of the church in Brno. Vlado's mother, before her marriage, had been a missionary worker for the Blue Cross, a revival movement within the Lutheran church of Slovakia.

Three times a day the Fajfrs conducted family devotions in their home. Mr. Fajfr would lead the morning and evening devotions, and Mrs. Fajfr the noon. During each devotion time a parent would read a particular Bible passage and explain it. Then the family would sing a hymn and pray.

Growing up Vlado attended Sunday school, young people's meetings and all regular church services. Indeed, as a young child he had been very religious. In later years his mother often recalled the times when he as a child would be soaring high in his swing and singing out, "Look, Lord Jesus, how good I am at swinging!"

As a teenager Vlado made a decision for Christ, but it soon became evident the decision had been no more than an emotional experience, unaccompanied by true repentance and faith. Then came high school and university when Vlado began to look on all he had been taught at church and home as utter foolishness. Surely it was as the professors said—"religion is only for weak people such as old women and sick men."

"It's for those who have no physical and mental strength to overcome the difficulties of their daily life," Vlado reasoned. "Such people use religion to escape to a world of imagination where they can avoid so-called 'sins'." To Vlado religious people used the term "sins" to refer to the joys and pleasures of this world.

From Vlado's point of view, the life of faith was very limited, seeking to hold its adherents in bondage through countless instructions and prohibitions. "You must do this and you can't do that." Such a life was not for him. He was young and strong and ready to live life to its fullest. He wanted to be free to pursue all the pleasure the world had to offer: theaters, cinemas, dancing, parties, girls, and whatever else might present itself to him for his enjoyment.

Mr. and Mrs. Fajfr, however, never gave up on their son. During all his years of rebellion, they prayed earnestly for him. Often when he would arrive home in the early hours of the morning from a dance or a drinking party, he would find his mother lying on her face, crying to God for him.

Untouched by the sight he would mutter to himself, "If it does her good, let her go ahead with her praying."

Still, at times he surprised himself with his own discontent. Although he associated with the highest society in Brno and was invited to many special events, he often found himself disgruntled over something as trivial as the pinching of a new pair of shoes.

"This has to stop!" he thought. "If my happiness is so fragile that a stupid pair of shoes can ruin my evening, there is something wrong with me. Wouldn't it be wonderful if I could learn to be happy no matter what happened to me—misfortune, prison, hunger. That would be wonderful. To be the master of my own fate."

Perhaps what Vlado needed was to cut down on his partying and start living right. Surely that would bring him happiness. He could start with his parents. He hadn't exactly been a loving son. He could start by showing them a little thoughtfulness. Next he could stop lying and disobeying. And surely if he didn't soon stop secretly visiting his best friend's wife, there was bound to be trouble. He could give that a try also.

Vlado did try to do these things, but after only a short while, he had to admit it wasn't working. He was back into lying, cheating on his friend, and bringing more heartache to his mother and father.

With his brief struggle over, Vlado consoled himself, "I can't change. I'll just have to make the most of it. What if my life doesn't bring me complete satisfaction. At least this way I'm not so troubled."

Though during his short-lived reformation Vlado had tried keeping the ten commandments, he still did not acknowledge the existence of God. Much of the teaching in the university had destroyed his childhood beliefs. He had studied Freud's psychoanalysis and Freuerbach's works. He was now of the opinion that God had not created man after all, but that man created God in his imagination and according to his own desires.

* * *

But, then had come the skiing holiday and his near brush with death. All his preconceived ideas about God and reality had been shattered. "How else can I explain it? It had to have been God's hand, intervening to save my life. And why? What thought have I ever given to Him?"

Under these circumstances there was no way that he could spend the last day of the year in revelry with his friends. When he brought up the news that he was going home the next day, they couldn't believe it.

"You can't leave now. Not before New Year's Eve." They tried to reason with him. "The fun has just started, and it won't be the same without you."

But leave he did. Quietly the next morning, without even telling his best friend of the incident on the mountain, Vlado Fajfr caught a train to Brno. He arrived in the city well after ten o'clock in the evening. He didn't have a key to the house, so he went to the church where he knew his parents would be taking part in the watchnight service.

Along the road he noticed the revelers, many of whom were already drunk, laughing raucously. Suddenly he saw as never before the emptiness. "What kind of joy comes out of a bottle?" he thought.

When Vlado entered the church service, he noticed the contrast. There were familiar faces of his childhood, whom he had despised, their faces radiating joy and peace. Here voices rose from hearts full of genuine love for their Lord—love, joy, and peace that he knew nothing about.

2
Lord, I believe!
Brno: 1936-37

The church in Brno was packed. As Vlado entered the building he noticed a difference. The atmosphere was charged with an energy he did not remember being present before.

Vlado had heard his parents and others tell stories of a little known Scottish evangelist who had begun preaching in Czechoslovakia a few months earlier. In the city of Kutna Hora, just south of Prague, God had so blessed the ministry of this evangelist that he had been invited to preach throughout Bohemia and Moravia. In each meeting the Lord manifested his power more forcefully, and the people attended in greater numbers. Before long the crowds outgrew the church buildings, and public halls and theaters were rented to accommodate them. God had poured out a spirit of revival upon His church in Czechoslovakia, and even the unsaved were thronging the meetings to hear the Word of God.

Mystified at the sight in the Brno church, Vlado thought, "Maybe the stories *are* true!"

* * *

The Scottish evangelist being used so mightily by God in Czechoslovakia was James Stewart.

Eventually, he visited Brno, invited by Vlado's father. It

was only natural that the evangelist should stay in the Fajfr home. And Vlado couldn't help but run into him at times.

What fascinated Vlado was that this young man had once aspired to playing professional soccer in his native land of Scotland. He had even been told by a professional club that they would sign a contract with him when he reached the required age. Before that day arrived, however, the Lord had saved James Stewart and called him to preach.

What kind of sportsman would give up such a promising career to become a preacher? Vlado determined to find out. He refused to attend the gospel meetings, but he liked the evangelist because he was young, full of fun and good humor, and was an exceptional soccer player.

One day Vlado invited him to play with the Brno team. Vlado, playing center forward, asked James to play beside him. James knew all the shots, had a good start with the ball, and was swift on his feet. Vlado was impressed. He and the evangelist quickly became friends.

Most of the time, James was occupied with the evangelistic meetings in Brno. As in other cities the Lord manifested his power so mightily that the largest halls had to be hired to accommodate the crowds. The whole city was stirred. In those days the Czechs were free to advertise and publicly invite people to religious services. Every streetcar had a poster covering one side, advertising the meetings and listing the subject on which the Scotsman would preach. The church in Brno experienced genuine revival, and many sinners came to know Christ.

Somehow in the midst of all God was doing Vlado was not moved. He was still clinging to the idea that the gospel was not necessary for a healthy young sportsman whose father was a wealthy bank manager. However, in his home Vlado could not possibly escape a confrontation with the evangelist.

"Tell me, Vlado. Are you a Christian?" James asked him one day.

The question did not surprise Vlado. He had expected as much. Many pastors and elders through the years had asked him the same question. It would be easy enough to answer yes—in fact, he was very tempted to do so.

Much to his surprise, however, he heard himself saying, "No, I am not a Christian."

"Why is that?" the soccer-playing evangelist asked. "Your mother and father are Christians. You know the way."

"The thing is," Vlado answered, "I like having fun. I like going to the movies. I like dancing and drinking parties. I like the girls. And sports—"

"I like sports, too," James interrupted. "Sports is a good thing, but Jesus Christ is far better. I know from experience that you will never be happy until He has first place in your heart and life."

After speaking further with Vlado about the claims of Christ on his life, James suggested he read his Bible seriously, beginning with the Gospel of John. Incredibly, Vlado agreed to do so. It was not as though he had never read his Bible before, but he had always read with a motive to find some contradiction so he could write the Book off as nonsense.

But this time, as he began to read the Gospel of John, he had a different motive. He really wanted to know the truth.

"When I read the Gospel of John," he would later say, "I saw two ball teams—Jesus and his boys against the Pharisees and the Sadducees. Jesus was the coach, Peter was center forward, Andrew was center half, James and John constituted the two backs, and Thomas was goalie. Judas was substitute. I must confess that at first I was a fan for the Pharisees and the Sadducees, and I wanted them to win. But as I read on, I saw that they did not play fair—and I was all for fair play even if I did not play fair myself! Eventually, I found myself cheering for Jesus' team."

* * *

It was while he was reading the Bible as he had promised James Stewart that Vlado went with his friends to the mountains for the Christmas holidays. This experience ended with the traumatic incident on the slope and a return home in time for New Year's Eve. Vlado was deeply convicted of sin and filled with a desire to find God.

A few days after he returned home, Vlado sought out his mother. "What happened when you were first converted? Was there a struggle before you finally gave in?" he asked.

Whatever his mother answered him at the time, it gave Vlado no peace. Inwardly his life was still in turmoil. But he continued reading the Gospel of John. He did not know until years later that his mother that night had discerned the working of the Holy Spirit in her son's heart and had spent the entire night on her knees in prayer for him.

Finally, on January 13, 1937, Vlado sat up late in the night reading. By this time he was in the ninth chapter of John which gives the story of the healing of the man who had been born blind.

The Spirit-convicted young man read, "He spat on the ground, and made clay of the spittle, and He anointed the eyes of the blind man with clay, and said unto him, Go wash in the pool of Siloam. He went his way therefore, and washed, and came seeing."

"Bravo," thought Vlado to himself, "Jesus has scored another goal!"

But Vlado soon saw that the Pharisees would not be so easily defeated. They obstinately refused to believe that this man had been born blind. Furthermore, they were enraged because Christ had healed the man on the Sabbath. This was a distinct violation of their religious convictions.

Reading of how the Pharisees pressed the parents of the healed man to say that their son had not been born blind, Vlado understood clearly what was taking place. These Pharisees were trying to intimidate the parents by implicating them in the work done to their son on the Sabbath.

As Vlado continued to read the Scriptures, his heart confessed, "I am just like these Pharisees. I see and know what a great work salvation is through Jesus Christ, but I refuse to believe it. I am the one who does not play fair. I am the hypocrite in this story!"

He read verse 34, ". . . And they cast him out. Jesus heard that they had cast him out; and when He had found him, He said unto him, Dost thou believe on the Son of God?"

Greater conviction gripped Vlado's heart as the Spirit enlightened him to the truth of the Scriptures.

The next verses hit even harder, "He answered, and said, Who is he, Lord, that I might believe on him? And Jesus said unto him, Thou hast both seen him and it is he that talketh with thee. He answered and said, Lord, I believe. And he worshipped him."

As Vlado read verse 38 his own heart unexpectedly echoed the words of the blind man, "Lord, I believe." Suddenly an unspeakable joy filled his heart with the blessed assurance of salvation. He was convinced of the existence of God, the living reality of Christ, and his need of the Savior.

He later testified, "I had such joy in my heart that my Savior Jesus Christ was living—and living in me—that I could have wished that the houses along the street where I walked would fall on me that I might immediately be with my Savior and Lord!"

> Something every heart is loving;
> If not Jesus, none can rest;
> Lord, my heart to Thee is given;
> Take it, for it loves Thee best.
>
> Thus I cast the world behind me;
> Jesus most beloved shall be;
> Beauteous more than all things beauteous,
> He alone is joy to me.
>
> When I hated, Thou didst love me,
> Shedd'st for me Thy precious blood;
> Still Thou lovest, lovest ever,
> Shall I not love Thee, My God?
>
> Keep my heart, still faithful to Thee,
> That my earthly life may be
> But a shadow of that glory
> Of my hidden life in Thee.
>
> — Tersteegen (trans. by Mrs. Bevan)

3
Vlado Fajfr, you have become a fool!
Brno: 1938

Immediately Vlado's life revealed that he was a new creature in Christ. He began to make things right with those he had wronged. Knowing the years of heartache he had caused his parents, he went to them to ask their forgiveness for his rebellion and waywardness. His tears of repentance and humility were met with tears of acceptance and joy on the part of his parents. The prodigal had come home!

Vlado then went before the church to ask forgiveness for his bad influence on the other young people, many who had been forbidden to have anything to do with him. He confessed his rebellious spirit in going against all he had been taught from his childhood and asked the leaders and members to pray for him.

Telling his friends of the change in his life proved to be Vlado's hardest task of all, but this he did, even in the face of incredulity and scorn. There was no doubt that this once proud, pleasure-loving playboy had indeed been changed.

Vlado's old friends did not exactly jump up and down with joy at the change they saw in their friend. As soon as they realized this was not just a passing thing as in times past, they began avoiding him. Even his favorite cousin with whom he had spent many a lively hour, upon receiving a letter of testimony from Vlado, replied, "I am sorry. I have lost a good friend."

When Vlado invited a former girlfriend to attend a gospel meeting with him, she reacted much in the same way. After sitting through a gospel message, the young lady arose in disgust, and, turning to Vlado before walking out, said, "Vlado Fajfr, you have become a fool."

Vlado was undeterred. For a while he continued going to the places he had frequented prior to his conversion. He wanted to share his newfound faith with his friends. Try as they might, they really could not figure out this new Vlado Fajfr. Why, only a few weeks ago he was all for having a good time. Now he was talking about Jesus and the Bible and a better way of life.

As he sat talking to them around a table in a mountain cottage, someone turned on the record player and music filled the room. Most responded and were soon out on the floor dancing. One girl stayed behind to keep Vlado company. He saw an opportunity to speak to her about the Lord.

Suddenly she interrupted him. "Why don't we dance while you tell me about this experience you have had?"

Intuitively Vlado responded—"There is no way I can tell you about the Lord Jesus and his power to save you from your sin while we are dancing the tango!"

With that, he left his old haunts, never to return.

Another change in Vlado's life was his attitude toward studies. Until his conversion, he had accomplished the bare minimum to get by and still carry on a life of sports, swimming, climbing, and partying. During the previous four years in the university, he had taken only the first required state examination. Overnight, he began to study seriously. The first part of each day he set aside for studying the Word of God and for prayer. The rest of the day, he gave to studying law.

Twenty-six months after his conversion, Vlado graduated with a Doctorate of Law degree from the University of Brno. He had passed his second state examination on civil, commercial, and criminal law, and the third exam on economic and financial science, and international law. During these months the country, in reaction to political events taking place around them, began mobilizing its military. Vlado became a junior officer in the Czech army.

"It's remarkable," one of his friends commented at the graduation ceremony, "the way the Lord helped you complete your studies in such a short time. You'd have never made it otherwise!"

Little did Vlado or his friends know at that time to what extent the Lord had worked. He received his degree in February, 1939. The following month Hitler with his German army invaded Czechoslovakia, and by the fall of that year all the universities in the country were closed down!

4
We were glad to hear your words of God's love
Brno: 1939

Vlado had always been a recognized leader and mover among his worldly friends. He began to steer his abilities into new channels. Studying the Word soon after his conversion, he realized that all those hours he had so despised in Sunday School and family altar were now paying off. The stories, the lessons, the memorized scripture—all came back to him with marvelous clarity. Soon he was sharing these truths with other young people in the church, encouraging them to study the Bible for themselves and to give a ready testimony for Christ wherever possible.

James Stewart had given Vlado several books, among which were two that captured his imagination. One was a book on revival and the other was an autobiography of a revivalist.

Stirred to action, Vlado exhorted the young people to earnest prayer for the unsaved in the church and for those with whom they brushed shoulders each day at work and school. Many of these young people had been converted during the revival that had swept their city the year before. They caught the burden and set aside at least an hour each morning when they would meet at the church to pray before going to school or work. They made a list of lost acquaintances for whom they would offer united and continual prayer.

Many had been saved during the days of revival, but there were still many who had been left untouched by the gospel. It was for these they now prayed, pouring out their hearts to the Lord in humble submission for salvation blessing. God answered the prayers. It was not long before one name after another of people who had been saved was scratched from the list. Almost every Sunday brought new conversions in the church in Brno. Many others fell under deep conviction of sin.

New life was poured into the church as the newly saved young people began eagerly telling others what the Lord had done for them. Vlado assisted them by arranging opportunities for them to witness.

A family in the church moved to a village six miles away. After visiting this family, Vlado discovered they had no gospel preaching church to attend. He left with a burden.

During a later visit with that family, Vlado asked the wife of the house, "What would you think about our starting a meeting in your home? We could invite your neighbors and the young people could sing and testify."

"No one would come," she replied. "We don't know anyone here yet."

"Don't you worry about that. The young people from the church will come and will go door to door inviting the villagers. They'll come; you'll see." Vlado was excited about the prospect of the young people witnessing to the villagers about the Lord.

Vlado went home and presented his plan to the youth group. With great excitement they went out by two's to each home, advertising the cottage meeting. The people came. They heard the joyful gospel singing, the fervent testimonies, and the good news of the gospel. And so it was that week after week the young Christians from Brno and the villagers met together in the home of the Christian family, the one group giving and the other receiving the precious word of salvation.

The Lord opened another door of witness for the young people through the advice of a Christian herbalist. He traveled throughout the area collecting plants for his business. Hearing of the enthusiasm of the young people, he approached Vlado.

"There is a village about forty miles from here where I came across a family reading their Bible. After speaking with them, I found out they wanted to know more about God. Do you think your young people would be interested—?"

"Interested?" Vlado interjected. "They would be overjoyed."

And so it was that a ministry was begun in that area that led to the planting of four or five mission churches under the leadership of the church in Brno.

Even after the Nazi invasion, there were opportunities to spread the gospel. The leading doctor of a sanitarium which treated lung diseases gave the young people permission to visit once a month and sing and testify. It was a wonderful opening to minister to people who had physical and spiritual needs.

However, one day as one of the girls was giving her testimony, she mentioned the name of the first president of the Republic of Czechoslovakia, Thomas G. Masaryk.

"We all know President Masaryk, how he was the 'Father of our Nation'," she exhorted. "Though he was loved and respected by our people, the most wonderful thing about him was that he believed in God."

Among the patients in the sanitarium was a German who reacted strongly to this remark. The patient thought this was a time to recognize the great Confederation of Nazi States, not a time to speak of nationalism. He was able to stir up enough trouble with the administration that they soon withdrew permission for the young people to visit and witness.

Naturally, they went to their knees in prayer. Vlado felt led to go directly to the head doctor and explain to him that their message was not political, but one that brought comfort and hope to the patients.

"We are sorry about this incident. Next time we come we will just sing," he said. This they did with Vlado giving a lengthy introduction to each song, explaining the words!

Three or four years passed before Vlado discovered the impact the young witnesses for Christ had made on some of the patients. One day while riding a train, he began to give his testimony to a man. Suddenly the man looked at him with surprise.

"Now I remember you!" he exclaimed. "Didn't you preach at the sanitarium a few years ago?"

"Yes, you must be talking about our young people from Brno," Vlado answered. "And I was there too, and said a word."

"I've always wanted to tell you how we were blessed by the singing and the testimonies, and we were glad to hear your words about God's love. I still remember your visits and the hope you left behind."

In another hospital for tuberculosis patients, the story was much the same. The majority of the patients had to lie day after day in body casts, sometimes for six or seven months, or even a year. During one service in particular the Lord spoke to hearts, so that at the end the young people were scattered throughout the ward praying with the patients. Some of the patients were actually born into the family of God, and later they started a Bible study among themselves.

This amazing witness continued while the Second World

War raged. The nation's political figures were bending under the iron hand of the Nazis. Czechs were torn apart, some being forced to fight with their German oppressors and others going underground to support the Allies. But these brave young soldiers for Christ had a much greater calling. They sang on crowded trains, in busy railway stations while waiting for their train, and often in the open-air in front of stations. In the midst of death and destruction, their message was one of peace and hope.

One young man confessed, "I was familiar with the gospel of Christ, but one day I heard your young people singing and testifying in the open-air. It was then, for the first time, I was impressed that I personally must do something about it, and I received Christ as my Savior."

In villages, in hospitals, in prisons, on trains, and in the open air, these young people spread the good news of the gospel that had changed their own lives and was now changing the lives of others. Surely these were days of blessing!

5
Vlado finds a bride
Gottwaldov: 1946

The war was over. The Lord had sustained the church through great trials and hardships. But, more wonderfully, He had added to His church in Brno, and raised up little mission churches throughout Moravia where people worshipped. It was certainly a time to praise the Lord.

About this time, the church in Brno, where Vlado had grown up and had worked with the young people, called a new pastor. Until now all the members had been involved in reaching out to the lost and taking part in the activities of the assembly. Many were involved during the week in the mission churches in the suburbs of the city, and only on Sunday did they all meet together to worship at the main church in the center of the city. Though a good man, the new pastor held to different ideas about the church. He had previously pastored a Presbyterian church, and he believed in a one-man ministry.

Vlado had spent all his life in that church, but now he realized that his time of service there was finished. There was so much to be accomplished, and his heart was bursting with the blessed truths of the gospel. He had to preach!

Knowing his own impetuosity, he first sought the counsel of an older and wiser Christian brother in his denomination. The brother had been a close friend of President Masaryk, often praying with him and advising him in his great task of leading the nation. After prayerful consideration before the Lord, Mr. Urbanek called for Vlado.

"I think it is time for you to leave Brno," he advised Vlado. "You should go to Gottwaldov. You have a special gift with young people. In Gottwaldov you will find many young people. Students. Young factory workers. It is a perfect place for your kind of ministry."

Gottwaldov was the new name for Zlin, a town practically owned by the Bata Shoe Factory. Bata was the largest factory in the world, and it sent products all over Europe and many other parts of the world. The factory employed thousands of workers, many of them young people seeking employment for the first time. What an appropriate place for someone with Vlado's gifts and vision to settle down!

Soon after he made the decision to move to Gottwaldov, Vlado made another equally important decision. During his worldly years before conversion, the vivacious young student and sportsman had been quite the "ladies' man." Since becoming a Christian, however, he had been completely caught up with earning his college degree and serving the Lord. He seemed to have neither time nor desire for the company of the opposite sex, except to win them to the Lord. Once he even considered taking a vow before the Lord that he would never marry and settle down to a normal life with a wife and family. But our Heavenly Father who directs the lives of His children had different plans for His servant.

Jirina Uherkova had been converted during the evangelistic meetings held by James Stewart in Vlado's home church in Brno. Transformed overnight, the young lady became a firebrand for God in the meetings and an indispensable help to the Scottish evangelist. Jirina was capable in her father's business, gifted in music, and a born organizer. Following the Stewart evangelistic campaign, Jirina dedicated her life in service to the Lord, and she began to seek ways to express this desire.

Before long Jirina took an active part in the young people's group led by Vlado. Whatever she thought about the youth leader at the time, he saw Jirina simply as one of the group.

* * *

An interesting thing then happened to Jirina. She had a dream. It was not one of those ordinary dreams which cannot be remembered the next day. It was a vivid dream, so real that it seemed to her as something which had already happened in the plan of God. In her dream, she was sitting again in church, but it was not her own pastor in the pulpit. Rather, it was a young Spirit-filled man under whose preaching the people were moved and awakened to the glories of the Lord Jesus Christ. As she sat listening, she suddenly recognized who this young preacher was. It was her own son, and he strongly resembled Vlado Fajfr!

So convincing was this dream to Jirina, that when Vlado visited her parents in Brno soon after his move to Gottwaldov, she fairly expected that he would declare his love for her and ask her to be his wife. Instead, he came and went without so much as a look in her direction.

Soon after Vlado's visit to Brno, however, his mind repeatedly turned to thoughts of Jirina—not idle thoughts, but thoughts that must be considered as coming from the Lord. And no sooner did he recognize his thoughts being from the Lord, than he found his heart longing for her, to be with her, to share his thoughts with her, in fact, to share his life with her. Without wasting time, he wrote a letter telling her what was on his heart, and asking her to be his wife. An answer was not long in coming from Jirina, accepting his proposal and committing herself to be Vlado's wife and companion.

Vlado Fajfr and Jirina Uherkova were married in November, 1946. The young bride joined her husband in Gottwaldov, ready to share in his life and ministry. For Jirina it was a dream come true!

Vlado already had found employment as a lawyer. Soon it became obvious that his work in the law office was simply a way to support his new bride. His primary goal in life was to tell others about Christ. With his usual gusto, Vlado threw himself into the work of reaching the young people of Gottwaldov. The Lord blessed his ministry richly. Many young people were saved. As news of Vlado's successful ministry began to spread, pastors outside the town, even outside his denomination, began to invite him for evangelistic meetings. He considered each invitation from an evangelical group to preach as an open door for getting out the gospel.

Soon Vlado's hands were full. He practiced law, regularly held outreaches for the young people of Gottwaldov, and traveled throughout the country preaching. And besides all this, he had a wife who shared in his love for the Lord and the Lord's work. For Vlado, life was good.

6

I got it from the Lord
Gottwaldov: 1946

Upon arriving in Gottwaldov, Vlado had been able to rent a one-room apartment. Housing was at a premium following the war, and he was happy to find any place to live. The apartment was crowded for the newlyweds, but they managed quite contentedly. Months later, however, when Jirina discovered she was expecting their first child, the need for a larger place became urgent. Humanly speaking there was little hope of getting a larger apartment. The two of them took their problem to the Lord.

Vlado and Jirina had heard stories and had seen the long line of people always waiting in the rental department of the town office. They knew of one family with several children who were living in one room but had been denied larger quarters. There were many others like them. What chance did a young couple with a new baby have? Praying for guidance and hoping someone would hear his case, Vlado visited the town office almost every time it opened.

Vlado had learned that in working with the bureaucracy an unconventional approach was often the best. With some difficulty he discovered the private address of the man in charge of rentals. Arriving outside the man's home late one Saturday evening, Vlado did not notice the sign on the front door forbidding business inquiries. What he did see was the hopeful sign of a light burning from a second floor window. He rang the door bell. No answer. Never one to give up easily and further assured that this prompting had come from the Lord, Vlado rang again and again. Finally the manager appeared at the door and immediately recognized Vlado as the young father-to-be who had been pestering him day after day for an apartment.

Instead of the angry words Vlado expected, the man said apologetically, "Do forgive me for keeping you waiting. I have been busy giving the children a bath and didn't hear the bell. Won't you come in?"

Within a short time the two men were carrying on a conversation like old friends, and before Vlado left, the manager promised him an apartment.

When Vlado finally arrived at home that evening, the caretaker of the building informed him that his wife was in labor and had already been taken to the hospital. All Vlado could think of as he hurried to see his wife was the Lord's perfect timing. The next morning he saw his baby daughter, Jana, for the first time.

"And to think, we will have a place to take her home to," Vlado said, as he began to relate the events of the past evening to his wife.

"But," Jirina later questioned, "why would he do such a thing? He doesn't even know us."

Vlado smiled, shrugged his shoulders, and said, "God!"

It was some time before they learned how the Lord had brought it to pass. At the time of Valdo's visit to the manager's home, a church elder and friend of Vlado's was vacationing in the mountains. The friend had felt such a sudden urgency to pray for the Fajfrs that he left his hotel room and went into the forest to pour out his heart to the Lord. He pled for a proper place for God's dear servants to live, a place that could be used in the ministry and would bring honor and glory to the Lord. How the Lord answered, abundantly above all Vlado and Jirina could "ask or think"!

* * *

Just like a new father, Vlado was dying to share his news. Off he went to find the new friend he had made the night before.

"Congratulate me!" he shouted. "I am the father of a wonderful, baby girl."

He then invited the man to attend church with him that evening. To Vlado's joy, he accepted.

On Monday morning the phone call Vlado had been expecting came. "Dr. Fajfr, this is the Town Office. You have been given an apartment on Hlukova Street, number 26," the voice on the other end explained.

Vlado was familiar with Hlukova Street. It was lined with small, rather unattractive houses. Pushing aside his disappointment, he hurried to the address to look at his new apartment. He searched but couldn't find apartment number 26. Finally he decided to ask someone for help.

"It's in there," someone told him, pointing toward a park at the end of the street. "One of those villas."

Finding it hard to believe, Vlado hurriedly sought number 26. There it was—a beautiful mansion-like house, complete with a large, private garden. What an incredibly beautiful place in which to live!

A Czech immigrant to California had amassed a large fortune and later returned to his homeland with enough money to build a large apartment building and a private house for himself and his family. Following his death, the man's daughter and legal heir immigrated with her husband to England.

According to Czech law, the house became the property of the government.

As Vlado inquired at the house he found the previous owner's mother still lived on the first floor. The vacant second floor had been allotted to the Fajfrs. The rooms were light and spacious, just the place to bring home a young wife and a newborn daughter.

When he told his co-workers at the law office, they could hardly keep the envy out of their voices. "Vlado Fajfr, how is it that you, a junior lawyer, have the finest apartment in Gottwaldov?" they asked.

Even his Christian friends were amazed and a little perplexed. "Aren't you ashamed to live in such luxury?" they asked. "Why, you even have two balconies!"

"I didn't choose it myself," he replied. "I received it from the Lord." And so he had.

* * *

For three years the Fajfrs enjoyed their lovely home. Then, unexpectedly the Town Office informed them that they would have to move. The house was needed for a kindergarten.

Vlado was preaching in Presov in East Slovakia when he heard the news. The government officials wanted to give him an apartment in a village some distance from the city. "Surely this couldn't be from the Lord," thought Vlado. "Much of my ministry is right there in Gottwaldov."

He called the church in Presov to prayer, asking them to pray in faith with him that his family would be given another apartment in the city. "We need an apartment with a large living room so we can continue holding meetings and Bible studies in our home," Vlado said, "and sufficient room for my family."

The Christians in Presov prayed. The Fajfrs prayed.

The Lord reminded Vlado how he had landed this apartment in the first place. He would need to go back to the Town Office and register a complaint concerning their decision to move him and his family to the country. The moment Vlado arrived in Gottwaldov, he went straight to the Town Office. He could not find the department for rentals. Someone told him that it had been moved, and that the department had a new supervisor.

"Upstairs, second floor," he was told.

On the stairs, Vlado stopped a man to ask directions. "Am I right for the rental office?"

"Sorry, that office is closed," the man said. "Actually, I am the supervisor and I am leaving for the day."

Vlado's face fell as his heart sank. Had he missed the Lord's prompting? He sent up a quick prayer to his Heavenly Father.

"I am disappointed," he replied slowly to the supervisor, "for I have come all the way from East Slovakia to meet and discuss something with you. My name is Dr. Fajfr."

To Vlado's surprise, the supervisor turned back to go up the stairs and led him into his office. Before long they were carrying on a friendly conversation. Vlado told him that he was a lawyer *and* a preacher of the gospel.

"Are you a Christian?" Vlado asked, a question he usually asked those he was meeting for the first time.

The man was taken aback. "The fact is, I used to go to church a long time ago," he said. "No, I don't go anymore. However, you shall have your place in the city."

Whether it was a kind heart or the desire of the man to get rid of the preacher, he rescinded the decision of the Town Office and gave Vlado residence in a new building. The new residence, too, was surrounded by a garden, and nearby was a lovely forest. The house had a large room for holding meetings and a smaller room which was perfect for a study. There was plenty of room for the Fajfr family. And it all came just in time, too, for before long Vlado and Jirina's first son, Daniel, was born.

The entire house was signed over to Vlado with the agreement that he would sublease part of it. The sublease clause was later removed and the Fajfrs were able to occupy the entire house until 1966.

7

He who risks nothing, gains nothing
Gottwaldov: 1949

"Have you ever considered going into evangelism fulltime?" asked Mildred Droppa, a young American lady doing missionary work among the children of Czechoslovakia. Vlado only recently had met Mildred and her friend, and with his usual enthusiasm for gospel work, he had introduced them to many of the local churches.

"How would I live?" Vlado immediately responded. "I have a family to support."

"Oh, I am sure I could arrange for a church in America to support you," Mildred assured him.

Vlado promised to pray about it.

Vlado's father opposed the idea. Even as a busy bank manager, he had time to be active in the Lord's work.

"Do your work as a lawyer to support your family," he advised him. "You can carry on your work as an evangelist in your spare time, just as you have been doing. Don't forget that Paul was a tentmaker."

"But I am not Paul," Vlado retorted. "Besides, I feel I'm wasting my time in the law office when I could be out doing the Lord's work. There is so much to be done and not enough hours in the day. I need more time."

After much prayer, Vlado decided to put out a fleece. He had only one brother, Joseph, who was his exact opposite in nature, looks, and personality. Vlado was vocal and energetic, but Joseph was quiet and thoughtful. When they were students, the entire family would celebrate if Vlado came home with passing grades. Joseph consistently made "A's." But Joseph was not saved. He had never seen the need. Vlado was concerned for Joseph. He prayed earnestly for his salvation, but still he saw nothing to encourage his faith.

Now, as he waited on the Lord for guidance concerning his future ministry, Vlado made a vow to the Lord.

"Oh, God, if you will save my brother, I will give my whole life to you in full-time evangelism—or whatever else you want to do with my life."

Much to Vlado's amazement, only a short time later he received the great news that Joseph had trusted Christ.

Without hesitation, Vlado left his law office behind.

"Czechoslovakia has enough lawyers to protect man's laws," he reasoned, "but God needs men to protect and declare His law!"

Few agreed. "Stop and think about it," his lawyer friends challenged. "You must be crazy to consider leaving a solid profession like law to be an evangelist. Have you lost your mind?"

* * *

They weren't the only ones who thought so. It was 1948, and the Communists had risen to power by overthrowing the existing Czech government. They flooded the country with a strong propaganda campaign on radio, in newspapers, in the schools, and in the universities.

"Religion is something that belongs to the past. It stops progress and drugs the people. God did not create man. Man created God in his imagination. During our generation, churches will become extinct as our people recognize that only scientifically-grounded, materialistic, atheistic, communistic ideology is reality. The coming generation will see the emergence of a new man. Gone will be the exploiters on the one hand, and beggars on the other. We will create a perfect society," the Communists said.

It all sounded so good. Many of the ideals appeared to be the very ideals God had in mind when He sent His Son into this world. People were impressed. All around Vlado his fellow Czechs were embracing Communism. Even some of the church members were deceived and became members of the Communist party, ignoring the fact that the very basis of this new ideology was "No God."

In this climate of political and social upheaval, Vlado made his decision. To those who objected, he replied cheerfully, "I'm willing to risk it. As the old proverb says, 'He who risks nothing, gains nothing.' Besides, our country needs the gospel now more than ever. It is the gospel that brings us near to God and to each other. It is the gospel—*not Communism*—that creates a 'new man.' We will never have a perfect society without Jesus reigning."

Realizing that he had a message far more revolutionary than Communism, Vlado dismissed every argument put to him.

Nevertheless, that was not the end of the matter. Hitler had closed all the universities during the Second World War, thereby creating a shortage of lawyers in Czechoslovakia immediately following the war's end. The new government made it very difficult to change professions, especially if one were a lawyer.

It appeared impossible to Vlado that he would be allowed to leave his job. Nevertheless, believing that the Lord would make a way for him if He had really called him into full-time evangelism, Vlado began to pray. Soon, in the providence of God, an old friend in his law office became secretary of the Communist Party of his district. Through the friend's influence, Vlado received his release.

There was another hurdle, however, facing Vlado. The new government did not allow full-time evangelists. They recognized only pastors as a profession. Furthermore, each pastor was under the control of a government agent known as the church secretary who granted permission to preach. Vlado questioned if the government would allow him to be an exception to the rule. Again he cast himself on the Lord.

"It is not possible that you will get this permission. Not when they are cracking down on everything religious," everyone told him. "Besides, the pastors only have permission to preach in their own districts. You wouldn't be allowed to travel as you have been doing. You wouldn't be under the jurisdiction of one particular church secretary."

Never afraid to ask his Heavenly Father for the impossible, Vlado was not deterred. Nor was he disappointed. The Communist government's church secretary gave him permission to be a pastor *and* an evangelist. A Baptist church in Kansas City, Missouri, supported him financially until the government finally put a stop to it.

Eventually permission was given in January, 1949, for Vlado to work throughout his country and in all denominations while supported by his own Czech Brethren Church. This blanket permission freed him to go wherever the Lord directed and was the only one of its kind.

The special liberties the Communist government granted Vlado to preach the gospel defied explanation, except that God was making the way for a distinctive ministry for His servant. And who could argue that Vlado himself was one of a kind!

8

We are witnesses of the power of the Holy Ghost
Gottwaldov: 1948

Soon after moving to Gottwaldov, Vlado had an extremely interesting conversation with a fellow lawyer who was also a zealous Christian.

"I have been hearing about the Keswick Convention in England," his friend said. "People from all denominations come together to study God's Word and to speak of the evangelization of the lost. Oh, if only we could have such a conference here. But, of course, it would be impossible."

"Impossible" was not a word in Vlado's vocabulary. Could they do such a thing? Why not?

Being an evangelist, he was acquainted with the evangelical leaders in all other denominations.

In the mid-nineteenth century, there had been a real move of the Holy Spirit which had reached the leading denominations. Many people were saved. In some cases, the new Christians chose to leave their cold, formal churches to form new churches. They called themselves Baptists, or Christian Brethren. Others chose to remain in their denominations, forming groups such as the Blue Cross within the Lutheran church in Slovakia and Snaha within the Presbyterian Church. Many such societies burdened for revival and for lost souls sprang up.

"What would happen," Vlado wondered, "if all these converted people were to come together for Christian fellowship and Bible study, and with intense desire to win lost souls?"

Vlado accepted the challenge. The challenge became a vision, the vision led to action, and action to results. In ordinary times such an undertaking would have been thought enterprising, but attempting such a thing at a time when the Communists were gaining more and more control was unthinkable. At least that's what most people thought. But not Vlado. To him each obstacle was an opportunity to prove the power and sufficiency of his God.

* * *

By this time the Communist Party had become powerful enough to take over the local government offices in the city. In one of their first moves they nationalized the BATA shoe factory. Vlado sought permission to use the factory dorms and beds left vacant by vacationing workers. Much to his joy, he discovered that the general director of the factory was an old high school friend from Brno. They had even gone to law school together, but had since lost contact.

"I can't believe it is you!" Vlado exclaimed. "What have you been doing all these years?"

After a few minutes of reminiscing Vlado told the factory manager about his conversion.

"And what may I do for you? Are you in some trouble?" the director asked.

"Oh, no. Not at all. Only I need your help. I need your permission to use the vacant dormitories during the month of June," Vlado requested.

Permission was granted.

Next Vlado would need permission from the city government to conduct meetings on a large scale. He knew this would not be so easy to obtain. With thousands of people coming from across the country for a full four days, officials were sure to be suspicious at the very least. Drawing on his experience as a lawyer, Vlado used his best diplomatic manner in presenting his proposal to the city council.

"Sirs, we wish to come together to unite the three Slavic language groups into a stronger bond. Like you, we desire to promote peace in all areas of national life as well as in the world. (He did not elaborate as to how he thought this peace could be reached!) We also would like to discuss the problems facing our society and how best to combat them. And foremost we wish to study and encourage ourselves in the faith of our great forefathers and national figures such as Jan Hus and Amos Comenius."

It must be noted that while the Christians in Czechoslovakia still look to Hus and Comenius as spiritual reformers whose lives and teachings were based on the pure Word of God, the Communists esteemed them highly as social revolutionaries. The most elementary history student has heard of the Bohemian Reformation under Jan Hus just one hundred years before the German Reformation under Martin Luther. After Hus was condemned by the Roman Catholic Council of Constance and burned at the stake in 1415, a great movement against the Roman Catholic Church began in the Bohemian and Moravian countries.

Hus had taught the people that Scripture only is the rule for faith and living. The people, including the ruling classes, turned to the Scriptures and to the teachings of Hus for guidance in their spiritual and practical life. The jewel which came out of the Czech Reformation was a church known as *Unitas Fratrum* (Unity of Brethren), founded in 1457. The chief characteristic of this church was a strong emphasis on purity of doctrine and practice as found in the Bible—seen in sharp contrast to the greed and debauchery of the organized religion of the day.

This new seedling of a church experienced almost two hundred years of persecution and resistance. Eventually, in 1620, the Hapsburg rulers prevailed and took all rights from the Czech Protestants. Thousands were forced to leave the country so that at one time 30,000 of them were scattered throughout Europe. Their spiritual leader, Amos Comenius, had been exiled along with them. The last bishop of the Unitas Fratrum, Comenius was a theologian of profound faith who sought to follow up the shepherding of his dispersed flock. He wrote many books to encourage their hearts and to keep alive the faith of the exiles and those left behind in the mother country. He was not only a strong patriot who fought to gain religious freedom for his people, but a well-known educator whose influence spread over the whole of Europe.

Such revolutionaries could not be overlooked even by the Communists. So Vlado pressed home his point. He left the presence of the officials to go home and pray and ask the other committee members to do the same—pray and wait. And when the answer came, it was affirmative. Permission had been granted.

Now, the hard work began—contacting the various evangelical groups, preparing a program, and arranging the speakers.

After much planning, praying, and anticipating, the first conference convened in 1948 with the theme, "Be Ye Reconciled to God." Two thousand people from across Czechoslovakia participated in this unprecedented gathering. Crowds were so large the committee had to finally hire a movie hall, a theater, a hotel meeting room, and a church hall. As usual Vlado was selected to make arrangements for the conference. It seemed no one could say no to him.

The theme for the second year was "God's Challenge to an Exemplary Life." Three thousand Christians represented all the revival societies from the large denominations as well as the free churches. The news of God's blessing on those who had attended the previous year had spread.

In April and May of 1950, when Vlado should have been getting things ready for the conference to take place in August, he was locked up in prison in Slovakia. In spite of Satan's opposition and with God's enabling, he was released in time to rush to Gottwaldov, secure the necessary permissions, and on the day appointed greet the thousands of people who converged on the town.

An official report of the 1951 conference revealed the blessed results of the meeting held that year.

> A conservative report about the convention held in Gottwaldov, now Zlin, from July 19-13, 1951: Approximately 3,000 visitors from all parts of our republic, Czechs, Slovaks, Poles, Hungarians, met as one family.
>
> One is reminded of the 3,000 on the day of Pentecost. It was our desire that the Holy Ghost should manifest His power among us. We are witnesses that the power of the Holy Ghost was real. He instructed and led us. He inflamed us to fervent prayer. He created a beautiful fellowship of love even while bringing many souls to salvation.

9

Watch, stand firm, be courageous
Gottwaldov: 1948-51

Attendance at the conferences soared higher each year. Fellowship around God's Word strengthened and encouraged the Christians who were facing intensified opposition to the cause of Christ by the Communist government. Indeed, such large numbers attending the conferences could not go unnoticed by *the powers that be*. By 1952 even Vlado Fafjr was not able to charm a permission from the authorities.

"It is harvest time and we need these people to work on the state farms to bring in the produce," the authorities argued. "This is far more important for the needs of our society than your religious meetings."

The real reason, however, was clear. The Communists feared the influence of the meetings. They feared anything they could not control. Besides, whatever the reason for their initial lenience, the Communists knew that the ideology of Christians and the ideology of the Communist Party were at opposite poles.

Open conflict with the Communists had begun in February of 1948, when they took power through a coup. They immediately began purging the old element in government. Those who did not agree with the thinking, methods, and goals of the Central Committee of the Communist Party were looked on with suspicion. Such people were *put away* either by imprisonment or death. Even members of the Communist Party who dared deviate from the main policy were not safe. They, too, were considered expendable.

And so it was that over those first few years of Communism, thousands were sentenced to prison or to death. Were there really so many enemies of the state? Often after much torture, these "criminals" were instructed in what they were to say in the courtroom. They each parroted the same confession, "I am guilty. I have been supported with money from capitalists in the West. I was being paid to overthrow the Communist Government."

This happened to one of Vlado's relatives. As a young man in high school, he enthusiastically embraced the doctrines of Communism. In college he was editor of a Communist magazine. Even when he qualified as a lawyer, he was so convinced of the Communist cause that he would defend a party member without charge. All this broke his parents' hearts. His father was a teacher in a Lutheran school and played the organ in church. His mother was a true born-again believer who had taught him Bible stories and how to pray as he was growing up.

When this man became the Minister of Foreign Affairs in 1948, Vlado visited him in his office in Prague. Vlado talked to him about using his position to help his country.

"Your mother taught you what was right and wrong when you were a young boy. You have a choice opportunity to apply these principles to this new government," Vlado reasoned with him. "You could really make a difference."

The only reply the relative gave was an indulgent smile, as though he were listening to idle talk.

Soon, however, upon returning from a visit to the United States where he had addressed the United Nations, he was arrested.

The judge asked him, "Are you a true Communist?" "I was never a true Communist," he replied. On reading these words in the newspaper, Vlado's father threw it on the floor. "That poor man has been tortured. He, of everyone in this country, believed in this regime." Sure enough, the man was sentenced to death and hanged. Several hours before he died, he wrote his wife, Lida, "I believe that in just ten years, you shall live in a socialistic Europe, and you shall greet it instead of me." His name was Dr. Vlado Clementis. Today in his hometown there is a statue erected in honor of him.

Such was the climate of 1952—one of great disappointment, disillusionment, and bankruptcy.

And so it was that those thrilling Bible conferences were over. They were held for four blessed years—that was all. But, oh, the profit that came from those days! As Paul would have said, "Much every way." Many came, invited by Christian friends and family, heard the gospel and were converted. In the year 1950 alone, the records show that 237 adults and 39 children came to Christ. That is not to mention the many who heard the gospel at a time when under ordinary circumstances they would never have heard. Over the years, Vlado constantly met brothers and sisters in Christ who joyfully testified that it was during one of the conferences at Gottwaldov that they received the Lord.

As to the believers, few realized at the time what strength and encouragement they would draw from these experiences in the coming years. Difficult days lay ahead. Yet, each one returning home, determined in his heart to stand true to the faith against all opposition. And, much to Vlado's satisfaction, he saw one after another stand up to the pressure from a government control that became heavier and heavier. Alone and yet united, these brethren were prepared to obey the instruction they had learned during the Bible conferences through the years, "Watch, Stand Firm, and Be Courageous."

10

What does this mean, Lord?
Rimavska Sobota: 1950

"Jirina, get some of those tracts out of my coat pocket and drop them as we pass by these people walking along the road," Vlado instructed his wife as they rode together on his motorcycle to the town of Rimavska Sobota.

It was April, 1950, and Vlado had just completed an evangelistic campaign in Slovakia. They were on their way to another town where he was to start meetings that night. God had been moving mightily and there had been an ingathering of souls. On this lovely spring day, both of their hearts were rejoicing in what the Lord was doing despite the opposition from the enemy of men's souls and the new regime. God was good.

And here was another opportunity to share the gospel. Vlado always carried tracts with him, usually using them as an opportunity to give his testimony. On this occasion, however, he had just a few left, and, being in a hurry, prayed that some of the leaflets left to the wind would be picked up by someone with a hungry heart. Thinking no more of it, the two of them arrived in Rimavska Sobota early, parked the motorcycle, and went into a restaurant for dinner. Near the end of the meal, Vlado pushed his chair back.

"Go ahead and finish your meal. I will check and see if any mail has arrived for us. I'll leave the knapsack here with you."

With that Vlado left the restaurant only to find a policeman standing beside the motorcycle.

"Is this yours?"

"Why, yes. Why?"

"Did you just come from Lucenec?"

"That's right. Is something wrong?"

"You had a pack with you."

"It is with my wife in the restaurant."

Vlado hurried into the restaurant, grabbed the knapsack, and motioned for Jirina to follow him. "Hurry, come with me. I think something strange is going on."

They handed over the well-worn knapsack to the policeman, and he opened it and started spilling out the contents. The bag contained some clothes, an assortment of tracts, several other pieces of literature, and a few personal letters.

"Come with me," the stern-faced officer demanded. A few minutes later the two found themselves at the police station. The police seemed to find a special fascination with the contents of their knapsack.

"What's this?" they asked, holding up several of the figures from the flannelgraph lesson Jirina had been using with the children in the recent meetings.

Vlado tried to explain. "That is a special method we use in the church to teach the children. This is the story about Paul in prison in the book of Acts."

"What do you mean, acts?"

"Acts in the Bible. It means activity, and after Jesus arose from the dead and went back to heaven, His disciples were full of activity, spreading the good news of the gospel. Some were even thrown in prison—"

"Yes, yes," the man sounded impatient. "But what is this on the back of the paper—those strange shapes of material."

He seemed to think it was some kind of secret code.

Until now, Jirina had kept quiet. Though nervous, she almost smiled. "Sir, those are just bits of flannel I paste to the back of the paper to make it stay on the special flannelboard which stands upright."

"Enough of that." The man questioning them turned to the bundle of letters.

"What we really want to know is why you have here letters from the United States and Britain."

Immediately following World War II, the people in Czechoslovakia had been left destitute from the bombing and from the Nazis confiscating everything for the military. Christians from the West had made contact with the Fajfrs and had started sending clothing parcels for them to distribute among the needy. That's what the letters were about. But to the authorities, it mattered not what was in the letters. The fact they were stamped with foreign postmarks was sufficient proof that these two harmless-looking people were spies.

"You wait here."

About thirty minutes passed before one of the policemen came back. He spoke to them kindly. "My wife is a member of the Baptist church where you are to preach tonight. I don't think you need worry. You will preach in Klenovec tonight as planned. I am sure they're going to let you go."

He went away and the Fajfrs continued to wait. Always the Lord had cared for them. They were His children and in His service. Surely He would deliver them as He had done before.

But God, under whose wings they had come to trust, had other plans for them.

The same policeman returned. "I am sorry, I was wrong. You are to be taken to Banska Bystrica to the magistrate there."

Just as it was getting dark, Vlado and Jirina were shoved

into a police bus. In front of them were four policemen in uniform and behind them four men who looked like important officials. Things appeared bleak.

"What does this mean, Lord?" Vlado whispered into the darkness to the One who had always been with him since the first day he trusted the Lord until now. He opened the Bible he always carried in his pocket and it fell open to words he could barely discern in the fading light. But he knew the story well. It was about Joshua the night before he and the Israelites were to capture Jericho. It read:

> There stood a man over against him with his sword drawn in his hand. And Joshua went unto him and said unto him, Art thou for us, or for our adversaries? And he said, Nay; But as captain of the host of the Lord am I come.

Vlado's heart was comforted. What they were about to face might not be easy, but the Captain of the Lord's host was with them. Praise His Name! He looked over at Jirina. He could tell she was praying. If only he could share what the Lord had given him, the Lord would minister to her too. Gently he patted her hand.

11
Oh, Lord, set me free!
Banska Bystrica: 1950

On arriving in Banska Bystrica, they were separated. It wasn't until days later that Vlado saw his wife again. Immediately, the interrogation began.

"When was this leaflet printed?"

"In 1947."

After further questioning another secret policeman asked Vlado, "When was this printed?"

"I told you, in 1947," Vlado repeated.

Vlado soon found himself in a chair surrounded by seven secret policemen. They took turns hurling questions at him, trying to wear him down. It seemed the ordeal would never stop. Then came the same question again.

"When did you say this leaflet was printed?"

"I think it was in 1947, just as I have told you," Vlado wearily replied.

With this, one of the interrogators slammed his fist into Vlado's face. "That's not the way to speak to an officer!" the man screamed. His companion struck Vlado with another blow, this time to the nose. Blood began to flow from his nose and cuts on his face.

Vlado thought, "I must remember not to say, I think. It seems to make them very angry."

The questioning continued for several hours. Two policemen left and two others took their place. Each time his answers did not please the policemen, they would strike him again, usually in his face or his head.

"Who gave you permission to distribute religious literature?" the officers asked.

"I did it according to our law. Our constitution guarantees us religious freedom," Vlado answered.

"This constitution you refer to is no longer valid," an interrogator replied, crushing Vlado's face with another blow.

Though he had little strength remaining, Vlado was then forced to stand, legs apart, arms over his head, and hands on the wall. Only with great effort could he retain his consciousness.

Then came the stunning accusation. "You are a spy for the USA and Great Britain!"

"That's not true. I'm not a spy," Vlado replied brokenly.

"You are a liar; you are a spy. We found the letters from the USA and Britain in your pack."

"I have told you, those letters are about clothing that we distribute among the poor. I am a simple preacher of the gospel."

"This distribution of clothing is only a cover-up for your real espionage work!" the police kept shouting. "We have all the proof we need that you are a spy."

As suddenly as the beating had begun, it stopped. Leading Vlado into an adjoining bathroom, the officers ordered, "Fill up the tub with water."

In his groggy state of mind, all Vlado could think was that they were going to drown him. Instead, the ranking policeman said, "The interrogation is over for now. Wash your face and you'll be taken to your celi."

Vlado gently tried to remove some of the blood caked on his hands and face. Then he went from one policeman to another, shaking hands and bidding them good night. His face showed no malice.

Embarrassed and chagrined, Vlado's accusers stood silently as they watched their unusual suspect walk away.

Jirina, Vlado found out later, was not beaten, but she was interrogated.

"Your husband has confessed that he is a spy," the interrogators announced. "He shall probably be condemned to death. You will never see him again. But, if you will give us some details about his work, we may be more lenient with him and give him only a few years in prison. We will even allow you to visit him. You see how important it is for you to cooperate with us."

Not knowing what exactly had happened to her husband or what he had said to them, Jirina cast herself on the Lord as never before and prayed that the Lord would keep them both faithful.

"You can do what you want to us, but the truth is that my husband is a preacher of the gospel of the Lord Jesus Christ. Our God will take care of us."

Apart from these few scanty details, Vlado never knew what took place with his wife. She never spoke of it.

* * *

At first Vlado was placed in solitary confinement. Understandably, the police did not wish others to see the extent of their *handiwork*. For the next three days, he vomited up everything, even water. After his release, a doctor told him that he more than likely had suffered a concussion, but at this point all he knew was that his mind was groggy and his body weak.

After a week, guards commanded Vlado to exercise with

the other prisoners an hour each day. During that first day of exercise, he was so exhausted after only thirty minutes that he begged to be allowed to sit down and rest. The guards refused to let him rest, and only with great strength of will did he drag himself around the courtyard.

Vlado was soon put in a cell with other prisoners. One of them noticed the bruises and cuts on his face and said, "They really beat you up, didn't they? Same with me. Three times I lost consciousness, but they didn't give up. They just poured water on me and beat me again. Try as they could, they didn't get anything out of me. What about you? What did you do to make them so angry?"

Later, Vlado was moved into a cell with only one other prisoner. Condemned as a smuggler, this man had already served half his sentence. During the day he worked in a nearby factory and in the evening he returned to his cell. Vlado told him that he was a preacher of the gospel and that was why he was put in prison.

One evening as he began to feel somewhat stronger, Vlado began to cry to the Lord. He felt sorry for himself because he was locked in prison when he could be out preaching and leading sinners to Christ.

Then it came to him. Tonight he was to have been preaching an evangelistic meeting in a Baptist church in Jelsava. He had planned to preach about Naaman, the leper.

Looking across the cell, Vlado saw his cellmate just finishing his evening meal. What a pity to waste a sermon! Besides, anything would be better than sitting around feeling sorry for yourself.

To the amazement of his companion, Vlado began preaching. "Naaman was a fine man! He was leader of the Syrian army. He was handsome, honorable, and brave. But—he was a leper. . . ."

The smuggler listened as Vlado explained how everyone has spiritual leprosy. "There is only one cure," the prison preacher said, "and that is Jesus Christ!"

Vlado had a captive audience. Obviously the man realized himself a sinner. He listened intently. Vlado finished the evening service by praying aloud for his new friend.

The next evening he preached another sermon. Again and again each evening, he preached one sermon after another.

Toward the end of the week, Vlado had preached and was ending his prayer when his friend began to pray. "Oh, Lord, you know all about me. I am a great sinner, but I have heard you died for my sins. I trust you as my Lord and Savior."

A great change settled over that prison cell. Mornings and evenings, the preacher and the smuggler shared precious times of fellowship. Vlado often testified later that he never before felt such a reality of the presence of the Lord as in those days.

In each cell he occupied, Vlado took his spoon and engraved on the wall the words of Psalm 50:15, "Call upon me in the day of trouble: I will deliver thee, and thou shalt glorify me."

During the day and the night he would cry to the Lord, "Oh, Father, you know that in August we plan to have another Bible conference in Gottwaldov. I have to get permission from the government and arrange accommodations with Bata factory. Then I must rent cinemas, theaters, and other halls for the meetings. The schedule must be prepared and there are so many other things to do. Oh, Lord, set me free! Deliver me from this prison for your sake."

1939: Vlado while in the military, soon after his graduation from the University

1947: Vlado and Jirina

1948: The first Sunday School in Gottwaldov was held in a school. Jirina, right, led this ministry.

1949: An open-air meeting at the international convention of Christians in Gottwaldov

1949: Vlado leads a service at the international convention.

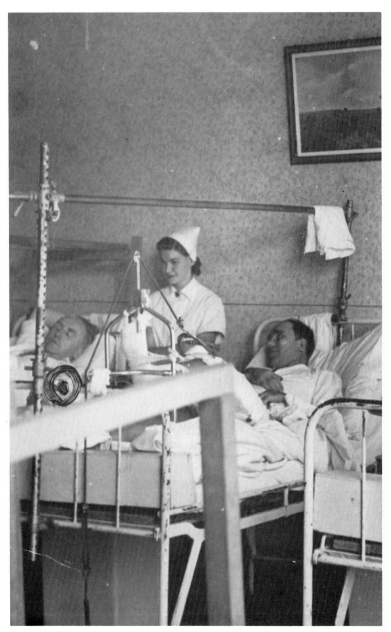

1956: Vlado, far left, "enjoys a vacation" in the hospital.

1956: When the Communists forbade youth camps, Vlado organized a "Holiday Family-Get-Together."

1970: Vlado, far left, leads another "unauthorized" youth camp.

1964: From 1962-65 the factory was Vlado's place of ministry.

1977: Vlado and Ruth soon after their marriage

1995: The renovated church building in Zilina stands as a testimony to the grace and power of God.

1995: Dr. Vlado Fajfr

12

Lord, I thank you
Banska Bystrica: 1950

"We are sending you to the steel factory in Podbrezova now that you have finished your time here. Your wife will work in the coal mines in Novaky. You will work during the day and in the evenings you will have the privilege of attending sessions where you will learn how to live and work in a socialistic society. If you perform satisfactorily in your work and your instruction, you will be free in six months. If not, you will stay indefinitely."

The decision of the five-member regional committee of the secret police stunned Vlado, who was being interrogated for the second time.

"Before we transport you to this work area, you must appear at the county office of the region where you were distributing religious leaflets without official permission. There you will pay a fine."

As Vlado and Jirina traveled to the county office to pay his fine, he started a conversation with the young secret policeman transporting them.

"What part of Slovakia do you come from?" Vlado asked.

"From Liptov," the young man replied.

"That's interesting," Vlado added. He knew that Liptov was located in a mountainous area in northern Slovakia and that during the counter-reformation, it had been left untouched.

It was a Lutheran stronghold.

"You must be from a Protestant, Lutheran background," Vlado said. "Do you attend church?" This he asked, knowing that being in the secret police, the man wouldn't be allowed to do so.

"I don't go to church, but my parents attend regularly," the policeman answered.

"I'm glad to hear that. I am a Protestant preacher and have often preached in your Lutheran churches," Vlado continued.

From that point on the policeman began to warm up to Vlado and Jirina. As they entered one town the policeman asked, "Would you like to stop and get something to eat? It will be a change from prison food. I'll wait here for you. I'm not worried about you escaping."

What a treat to purchase a couple of small pastries and two soft drinks, Vlado and Jirina thought.

Having eaten their food, the two rejoined the policeman to continue their trip. No sooner had they begun than Vlado asked the policeman to stop again, this time at a newsagent where he bought ten postcards and stamps. The three then continued their trip to the county office.

* * *

While Vlado and Jirina were waiting to see the judge, they sat in the corridor of the county office. In the providence of God, one of Vlado's cousins who was a county hygiene physician unexpectedly walked out a side door. Seeing the Fajfrs, he rushed over to them.

"Where in the world have you been?" he asked. "We have been making all kinds of inquiries trying to find you."

It was in the church of this cousin that Vlado was to have

been preaching and in his home that they would have stayed. The church, Vlado was told, had been packed with at least five hundred people waiting for him to arrive while all the time he had been sitting in a jail cell! As Vlado tried to explain the situation, the policeman motioned for them to stop talking.

"I am in prison," he managed to whisper before being taken away.

Later in court, when it came their turn, the judge's voice boomed across the courtroom, "I must punish you very strictly for this religious activity of distributing religious propaganda here in Slovakia. You must return to prison."

"But, your Honor," Vlado protested, "I was told I had only to pay a fine."

The judge then leaned forward and whispered, "Do you know Dr. Manica?"

Vlado was startled. "What are you saying?" he asked.

The judge gave him a knowing nod and waved his hand for the next case.

The Fajfrs learned later that the cousin whom they had met in the hall had immediately tried to secure their release. He spoke first to the chief of police, but without success. Then he went to the home of their uncle, a general in the Slovak army and a strong Communist who had a great deal of influence in the town. Even the uncle's efforts had not availed. The chief of police in Banska Bystrica remained adamant, "This man and his wife are going to labor camp. Nothing can stop this."

Apparently giving in somewhat to the pleas for mercy, the police chief agreed to hold Vlado and Jirina in the local jail for a short period of time before sending them to labor camp. This encouraged Vlado because he knew that once he and his wife were sent to the factory or the mines, release would be almost impossible.

Fortunately the couple were put in a cell together. After only a short time in the jail, Vlado, looking through the barred window of their cell, spotted a boy of about six or seven years old. The young lad, who was the jailer's son, crawled onto a stack of wood and peered into the window to see who the latest occupants were.

"Young man, do you think that if I were to give you some postcards that you could mail them for me," Vlado asked.

The little fellow nodded his head. "I can do it. I'm big for my age."

On each of ten postcards Vlado wrote, "I am in prison, condemned to a labor camp, but I believe when the church shall pray for my deliverance, like in Acts 12, I shall be set free." He addressed the cards to churches where he had ministered in Slovakia and in Moravia, knowing they were praying people. After putting the stamps on them, he called the boy.

"Son, here are three postcards. Mail these and then come back to tell me you have done it."

A few minutes later, the boy returned. "I mailed your cards," he boasted.

"Now here are three more. Do the same," Vlado instructed.

Later he gave him the remaining four cards. By giving the cards to the lad in this manner, Vlado felt confident the boy would be more careful with them and would not lose one along the way.

All at once Vlado felt impressed to write a letter to a friend in Gottwaldov. The man was a member of the Communist Party, but during Vlado's days as a lawyer the two had become friends.

He found a piece of paper and began to write:

Dear Honorable Mayor:
    I am in prison, condemned to a labor camp. Please help me if you can.

Yours truly,
Vlado Fajfr

Searching his pockets, Vlado found an envelope. Then he lifted the lapel of his jacket and removed a ten crown note he had pinned underneath it for such an emergency as this. He addressed the envelope and attached the money to it with a safety pin.

Again Vlado called for the young boy who had dutifully mailed the postcards for him earlier. "Here is a letter I want you to mail. The ten crown note will take care of the postage."

Then he and Jirina prayed, committing all of the pieces of correspondence into the hands of Him Who works all things according to His purpose.

Soon God began to work in a most unusual way. The mayor of Gottwaldov later told Vlado the story. "When your letter arrived, I wondered what I could do since your sentence was received from a regional office, not a local one on my level. Then I remembered the District Chief of Police of southern Moravia who was also a member of Parliament and had great influence. I knew he was acquainted with you. Perhaps he would help. I contacted him and his reply was, 'Do all you think best for Dr. Fajfr's release, and I will endorse it. He is a good man.'

"With the help of a lawyer, we wrote this letter:

To the District Chief of Police in Banska Bystrica,
    Dr. Vlado Fajfr is a well-known cultural and peace worker. We cannot begin to tell you all that he has accomplished in our town. Not only has he worked for peace here in Gottwaldov, but in the entire region of southern Moravia. If he is not set free

immediately, we shall appeal to the highest power in the country.

>Signed:
>Chief of Police
>South Moravia

"We called the Banska Bystrica regional office, read them the letter, and then sent it registered mail."

But why would such an important official in the Communist Party be willing to help Vlado? Why would he even remember him? The answer went back to a meeting they had two years earlier. In 1948, after the takeover, the secretary of the Communist Party—this man—visited Vlado's law office.

"Dr. Fajfr, we've heard all about you. You already have a reputation of being a man of your word, a man of integrity. We need such men in the Communist Party. I hear that you, too, are for social justice and for peace. Am I right?"

With this introduction he laid in front of Vlado an application for membership in the Communist Party. Vlado was shaken. He had heard all the propaganda about a new society being created, a "world without war." It would be a society that would stand for justice and peace in exact opposition to the capitalist nations which were controlled by greed and which wanted war. On the other hand, in this "new society," anyone who expressed doubt as to the validity of such claims would be considered a traitor. He knew that his refusal to become a member of the Party could mean a loss of his job at the least, and at the most he might be forced to work in the coal mines.

"Mr. Secretary," Vlado found the courage to say, "I understand the ideology of the Communist Party is atheistic. We are constantly being told, 'religion is the opiate of the people.' But I believe in Jesus Christ who has changed my life, and I try to live according to the Bible. You have to admit I wouldn't make a very good member of the Party." And with those words, he kindly but firmly refused.

The Secretary later repeated what had happened to the mayor of Gottwaldov, and added, "The rest of the lawyers in this town are cowards. They've joined the Party for fear of losing their jobs. Only Dr. Fajfr is strong enough to stand up for what he believes. That's what I consider a man."

Now the Secretary was sticking out his neck for this "man." It took a few days for the word to filter down, but the day came when Vlado and Jirina were released. Their motorcycle was returned, though somehow in the intervening time it had been damaged. After getting the necessary repairs done to it, they started for home.

Together they reviewed the strange events. The interrogation. The conversion of a smuggler. The young policeman from Liptov. The cousin. The county judge. The jailer's son. All had worked together for their release, and somehow for the glory of God.

The sun was just going down, and Jirina commented, "I'll be glad to see the children again. Poor things, I'm sure they have been worried. But right now, I'm cold."

"We pass through Vsetin this way. Why don't we stop at the pastor's home and get you some warm boots and a jacket," Vlado suggested. "We can still make it home tonight."

It was already dark when they arrived at the church. The apartment where the pastor's family lived was dark too, but they could see a light shining from the church hall.

"I wonder what's going on."

"I don't know. It's not a regular service night. Do you think someone could be cleaning the hall?"

As they entered the hall, Vlado and Jirina found twenty-five people on their knees, pouring out their hearts to the Lord in prayer.

"Oh, Lord," prayed one dear sister, "We are trusting you to set the Fajfrs free. They are your children and in your care. We are believing you that you are going to answer our prayers."

With that Vlado lifted up his voice in praise, "Lord, I thank you that you have heard this dear sister's prayer and by your miraculous power, you. . . ."

Vlado later said he understood exactly how Peter felt when he interrupted the prayer meeting in the home of John Mark's mother! Oh, the disbelief! Then the joy and thanksgiving! The whole prayer meeting was disrupted as brothers and sisters embraced one another and begged to be told how the Lord had answered their prayers.

The believers told how the pastor had received Vlado's postcard and then called the church to prayer despite the danger connected with meeting at undesignated times. They had been meeting every night to pray specifically for the Fajfrs and their deliverance.

Vlado told them of the strange sequence of events that led up to their release.

Privately, Vlado wondered, "What would have happened if I had not had the courage to turn down the offer of the Secretary? Would he have bothered to write Banska Bystrica on my behalf?"

It struck him that in all likelihood, he could have received an even stiffer sentence for being a card-carrying Communist giving out religious tracts!

Later, Vlado's cousin told him the judge had said, "We've never had such a case before. I was impelled to release that man and his wife."

And so it was that Vlado was released just in time to make the necessary arrangements for the Bible conference in Gottwaldov. God is always on time.

13

All things work together for good
Gottwaldov: 1956

It seemed there were never enough hours in the day. The ministry in Gottwaldov was enough to keep the average pastor busy. Besides that, Vlado felt especially responsible for the small missions, or *house churches,* that had sprung up in villages around Gottwaldov as a result of his many outreaches. Too, each year brought more offers from churches around the country inviting him to come for evangelistic services. Jirina and the three children felt as if they never saw him. But there was no use telling Vlado to slow down—not when there was so much to be done.

On one particular Wednesday afternoon in 1956, Vlado started on a trip to the town of Uherska Brod where he was to speak to a small group of believers at a Bible study. Speeding along on his motorcycle, Vlado became preoccupied with the glorious truths he wanted to share with the Christians in Uherska Brod. A light rain began to fall, but being used to traveling in all sorts of weather he thought nothing of it.

Approaching an intersection, Vlado glanced to the right to check oncoming traffic. A car nearing the intersection appeared to be slowing down and yielding the right-of-way. He looked to his left. No one was coming so he continued ahead. Suddenly Vlado realized the oncoming car was not stopping. It was coming straight toward him. Slamming on his brakes and skidding on the wet pavement, Vlado struck the car and landed under its left wheel. When he tried to get up, he couldn't move his leg.

So, instead of speeding away to Uherska Brod to preach the gospel, he was sped away in an ambulance to the nearest hospital.

After inspecting the fracture, the doctor announced the verdict to his disgruntled patient.

"This is not a simple fracture. The bones have overlapped. You will need to stay in the hospital for three months, flat on your back with your leg in traction." With that sobering pronouncement, Vlado was taken to the operating room where the doctor bored a hole through the bone just below the knee and attached an instrument with a twenty-pound weight.

Vlado was puzzled. How could this happen to him? He had been on his way to serve the Lord, and indeed his whole life was given over to serving the Lord. People were waiting for him.

Vlado found himself arguing with the Lord. "Dear Father, How could you allow this accident? I'm your child. You know all I've got to do. I don't understand."

But God has His ways of getting the attention—and devotion of His children. Often seemingly at the most inconvenient time the Lord allows them to be laid aside, usually for their own profit. Mrs. Charles Spurgeon, wife of the well-known London preacher, spent years as an invalid. As she lay on the bed of affliction, she wrote:

"If we can only get firmly fixed in our hearts the truth that the Lord's hand is in everything that happens to us, we have found a balm for all our woes and a remedy for all our ills. We are too apt to look at the visible, second causes, and to forget that our God has foreseen every trial, permitted every annoyance, and authorized each item of discipline with this set purpose: 'Whom the Lord loveth He chasteneth'."

The Lord not only chastens those whom He loves, but He adjusts them to the circumstances which He uses for chastening. So it was with Vlado. Soon after being transported to the hospital ward, he looked around the room curiously. There were eleven other patients in the ward, most of them in circumstances similar to his.

"Yes, Lord," he whispered, "I see what You have for me. Here's my next evangelistic meeting, and I don't have to worry if they will come every night. A full house! But how shall I reach them? What do you want me to say?"

The following evening, after the nurse turned out the lights, Vlado cleared his throat and began.

"My fellow-sufferers," he said. "I think it would be a good thing if we would encourage our hearts from God's Word which never fails. God's words are true and they apply to every situation, especially to us as we lie helplessly here in this hospital." He went on to explain the Lord's Prayer as most of the patients were familiar with the words.

"'Our Father, which art in heaven.' God is in heaven. He is holy and mighty, but He tells us to pray to Him as 'Father.' However, we don't appreciate and trust Him. We live our lives without Him, far from Him, as did the prodigal son. You know this story. . . ."

And so Vlado plainly explained how every man is a sinner. He spoke just a few sentences, and prayed a short prayer, committing the men to the Father's care. The next evening he spoke on the second phrase of the Lord's Prayer, "Hallowed be Thy Name." Each night following he spoke and the men quietly listened. After he finished the Lord's Prayer, Vlado began with the Ten Commandments. As on the first night, he concluded his words with a short prayer.

One night, to test his audience, Vlado remained quiet after the lights were out. Suddenly a voice broke the silence, "Are we not to get our speech from the Bible tonight?"

"If that's what you want, I'll be happy to continue," Vlado responded thankfully.

In the mornings Vlado studied the Psalms for his own private devotions, taking one psalm each day and meditating on it. He reveled in the leisure time he had to read and think and pray, remembering his recent heavy schedule. As the days went by, he realized more and more how badly he had needed this time to rejuvenate his spiritual life. God, in His wisdom, had given him just the right kind of vacation.

One day, a new patient was brought in. He was the official organist for the local Roman Catholic church. That evening as Vlado began his usual devotions with the men, the new patient began to distract the other men by coughing repeatedly, clearing his throat, and carrying on a conversation with the patient in the bed next to him. He tried everything to keep the patients from hearing what Vlado was saying.

Finally, the man rudely interrupted Vlado and addressed the other patients. "You know you shouldn't be listening to this preacher. Everyone of you is supposed to be a good Catholic. But this man doesn't belong to our church. He's a heretic!"

The man's comments greatly upset Vlado, but he did not respond to them. The ward soon quieted down and all seemed to be asleep except Vlado.

"What should I do?" he wondered. The men had been listening so well, and seemed so receptive. Now this one troublemaker had come in, and to Vlado it looked like he would be forced to stop his witness. It just didn't seem right. After praying, Vlado felt better. Tomorrow, he would put it to a vote. If the majority wanted to continue the evening talks, he would. If the majority opposed, he would be quiet. With that, he dropped off to sleep.

The following morning, Vlado discovered his psalm for the day was Psalm 40. As he read, verse four seemed to jump off the page. "Blessed is that man that maketh the Lord his trust, and respecteth not the proud, nor such as turn aside to lies."

Here was a word from the Lord. Vlado wasn't the heretic! He had made the Lord his trust. It was the other man who was proud and full of lies. By the time he had finished his quiet time, he had made up his mind.

"No voting," he concluded. "No democracy. I'm going to obey God's Word and not give respect to the proud."

That night, after the lights were turned out, Vlado addressed the men. "My friends," he began, "you know I have been fair with you. I haven't tried to get you to join my church or adhere to my creed. Instead, I have spoken to you simply about the faith that is in Christ Jesus, about His death for our sins, and about His resurrection—simple truths from the Bible. This Jesus Christ is the Savior for Jews, Gentiles, Protestants, and yes, even Catholics. So we are going to continue talking about the parables. Tonight we will deal with . . ."

And so Vlado boldly carried on his witness. The new patient, Mr. Malina, tried again to disturb the devotions, but the rest of the men paid little attention. Vlado was encouraged.

The following day one of the nurses came into the ward. "Mr. Malina," she said clearly for all to hear, "You are to be moved to Ward Three."

The men all looked at one another. It was well-known that Ward Three was the room for patients with open wounds. Often the infected wounds gave off a terrible odor. Everyone tried to stay clear of Ward Three.

As soon as the nurse left the room, Mr. Malina declared,

"I won't go. They can't make me."

Later the nurse returned to the room and was surprised to see Mr. Malina still lying there. She spoke to him as though he were a naughty child.

"Mr. Malina, we have a patient in the operating room who has just had a very serious operation. The only bed left is in Ward Three and it would be dangerous for him to go in there. You, however, are not so sick, and there is no danger of you getting an infection."

"I'm not leaving here," Mr. Malina protested adamantly.

The nurse left and in a few minutes, she returned, accompanied by the head nurse. She announced with a voice of authority, "Mr. Malina, in the name of the head doctor, you will go at once."

This time there was no refusing. As the man passed Vlado's bed, his glance seemed to say, "This is my punishment for disturbing your evening services."

The other men seemed to agree because from then on there was a strange hush during the evening devotions. Ten days later when Mr. Malina was allowed to return to the ward, Vlado found him subdued.

Three months went by, Vlado's leg healed, and he was dismissed from the hospital. For the first few days he had to lie in bed at home, but it was good to be in his own bed with his family around him once again. Gradually, he was able to get up for a few hours each day and walk around on crutches. He became anxious to get back into meetings again. For the first service, he would only have to walk downstairs to the large living room where the regular Sunday evening service was held.

As he rested before the meeting, he meditated on what he would say. Romans 8:28 was the perfect text. Now he could see God's hand in his accident—the rest, the time to meditate, the witness with the men in the ward. He knew also that the time spent in the hospital had been a time of discipline. It had all "worked together for good" because he loved the Lord and had been called by Him. It was all so clear.

With his mind on his message, he sat up and reached for his crutches. Looking at his feet rather than his crutches, Vlado started toward the door, caught one of his crutches in the heating vent, and fell back against the bed with a thud. In dismay he heard something snap in his right leg.

The ambulance came. Vlado was quickly carried back to the same hospital, back to the operating table and the same doctor, and back to another three months of lying flat on his back with his leg suspended! This time, however, the fracture was more complicated than before. The bones in his leg were overlapped and a steel pin inserted. Then a twenty-five pound weight was again attached.

"I'm sorry this has happened, Dr. Fajfr," the doctor sympathized. "I know this is very discouraging for you."

"It's all right, Doctor," Vlado said cheerfully. "I have a God Who is in control. Have you ever read that verse in the Bible that says, 'All things work together for good to them that love God'?"

"I can't say that I have," replied the astonished doctor.

"Well, I'm one of those people." Vlado smiled and pointed to his leg. "I'm right where He wants me to be. You don't have to worry about me being depressed."

Later the same doctor told Vlado that he had never before seen a patient with a re-fracture who did not suffer from discouragement and depression. Dr. Fajfr was the first he'd seen take it in stride. Of course, it was the perfect lead for Vlado to tell the doctor about the grace of God and its sufficiency. It was one of many times he was able to speak to him about the claims of the Lord Jesus Christ on his life.

Imagine the comments and good-natured teasing when Vlado was taken into his old ward. "You are a man full of troubles," one man called out.

"You're wrong," Vlado shouted back. "This is my opportunity to finish my sermon! I hope you're all ready."

The men in the ward appeared happy to continue with their nightly talks. Vlado settled in to the routine once again, looking for opportunities to make this second time in the hospital count as much as the first. Every day seemed to bring an opportunity to share something of his faith.

In the ward next to Vlado was a patient who had tried to commit suicide by jumping from a third-floor window of the hospital. The patient was an independent farmer, meaning that he had refused to become a member of the Communist Agricultural Cooperative Union. As such, he had no one to look after things while he was in the hospital. Depressed over the thought of losing everything, he attempted to kill himself.

Usually, patients in his condition were sent to a mental hospital. In this case, however, the doctor to whom Vlado had witnessed brought the man to Vlado and arranged for him to occupy the adjoining bed.

"Dr. Fajfr, I have here a sick sheep for you. Care for him like a good shepherd," the doctor said.

A combination of the good atmosphere in the ward, and Vlado's encouraging words wrought a change in the man. He became quiet, his health slowly returned, and after two weeks he was well enough to go home.

Vlado's second three months in the hospital passed quickly, and he was soon dismissed. This time, however, he was more cautious with his crutches. Before long he was back to his usual athletic self, swimming, skiing, and playing soccer with the young people. In fact, he could do anything he had done before the accident.

Looking back on those months in the hospital, Vlado realized it was definitely not wasted time. He often remembered with envy the times of quiet fellowship with his Lord. He realized that the Lord enjoyed this fellowship so much that he had prolonged it from three to six months!

Later, in expounding Romans 8:28, he would say, "Yes, 'all things work together for good to them that love God,' it is true. But I have to add that in our life of faith, it is not so much the 'good things' or pleasant things which work together for good, as much as the unpleasant things, the tribulations, the chastenings, persecutions, sorrows and hardships—these, of all things, work together for our good!"

14

A witness wherever he goes
Gottwaldov: 1962-65

Suddenly Vlado understood. This was not about a parking ticket.

The tone of the police official was confidential. "You have connections. You know what the people are saying, what they are thinking about the Communist government and about Marxist doctrine. And you—you, too, are for social justice and world peace. We could work together. All we ask you to do is tell us the truth about what is going on."

Not waiting for a reaction the official continued to explain how it would work. Vlado would be cooperating with the secret police. They would arrange to meet him at a pre-appointed place and time—in a park, a restaurant, or some public place.

"But this will have to be kept strictly confidential. No one must know!" he warned.

It had all started a few weeks earlier when Vlado received a summons to the police station, charged with parking in a no-parking zone. A few days later he received another summons to have his driver's license checked. The second summons raised his suspicions. Could this be connected with the letter that came the previous month accusing him of collaborating with the Nazis in World War II?

Of course, that was nonsense. He had made a trip to Vienna

during the war years, it was true. But he had gone as a lawyer to study the German law concerning anti-aircraft. He had been sent by officials in Brno so they would know what to do in the event their city was bombed. Now the secret police were using this to put fear in his heart, he was sure. How did it all fit together?

He soon found out.

As he was leaving the office of the city traffic police, he was stopped.

"Are you Dr. Fajfr?" a man asked him.

Vlado nodded.

"Come with me."

He was led into a room where an important-looking man was seated behind a desk. "I wish to ask you a question. Is it true you were the leader of the 'Family Holidays Get-Togethers' in Valassko?"

"Yes, I was."

"Very interesting," the man commented, holding on to his words as though he was about to say more.

Vlado wondered how much the man knew. He had done the best he could to camouflage the youth camp by naming it "Family Holidays Get-Togethers" and by inviting families with young children to attend. His work with young people always irritated the Communists, who saw the young people as their particular mission to train in Communist ideology. For that reason youth camps and all such activities were forbidden.

Vlado waited. What would they accuse him of? Did they have proof? He remembered again the dirty cell in Banska Bystrica, but he knew he must not allow fear to show in his eyes. That is what they wanted. Everything was calculated to create fear and submission in his heart. They would not win.

It was then they brought up the subject of cooperating

with the secret police. As always a sweet peace flowed into Vlado's heart. Suddenly the humor of the situation hit him. Hiding a smile, he turned to the men in front of him.

"You must be joking!" he said. "You see, you don't know my wife. She's very observant. You have been blowing cigarette smoke on me the whole time I have been sitting here. When I get home, the first thing my wife will say to me is, 'Where have you been? You smell like you have been in a cheap tavern. Tell me the truth.' And I will say, 'I can't tell a lie. I have been with the secret police, and they have asked me to be a confidant for them.' You see how it is; it would never work."

Strangely, Vlado was allowed to leave the station though he could tell the police official was none too happy. When he confided in a friend as to what had taken place with the Czech KGB, he was warned, "You wait and see. It won't take them three months to take away your permission to preach."

The friend's prophecy proved correct. Within three months, Vlado received a letter from the regional office of the KGB stating that his pastoral work and "especially the training of young people is against the public interest. As of December 31, 1961, your permission to preach will be terminated."

He was told that he could do one of three things. He could go to the forest to cut down trees as a lumberjack, work on a state agricultural farm, or become a factory worker doing piece work. Going back to practicing law was not an option.

Jirina and he discussed the situation. "I could easily get a job. You know how good I am with languages," she reminded him. "Don't forget that before I married you, I used to travel for my father's business. I've had a great deal of experience in the business world."

"But the children are still small. Especially young Mark.

How would he manage without you?" Vlado insisted. "I have to go to work somewhere, so who will take care of them? It's best you stay home, and we will trust the Lord to meet our needs as we have always done."

Being fifty-one years of age helped decide which job to choose. In January, 1962, Vlado Fajfr—preacher, evangelist—began a new career making precision instruments in a manufacturing company. The first day on the job, he wondered if he would ever learn to run the machine well enough to support his family.

At first, because he was paid by the piece and the job was so foreign to him, he came home with very little money. At times he worked up to sixteen hours a day only to find there was hardly enough money to buy groceries. One day, when he was especially discouraged, a neighbor slipped him some money, though Vlado had told no one of his family's need. Later, as he became more accustomed to the work, he was able to provide quite well for his growing family. In fact, he discovered that the machine they had put him on was one of the best paying in the factory! God had worked everything out again.

Vlado found another blessing in working in the factory—time to read and study his Bible. Often there was a long interval between the time he finished one piece and the time another arrived. During this time he often prepared his sermons for the next Sunday.

It is true he was not allowed to preach, but his church had received permission for another man in the congregation to take his place. This brother in the Lord, who worked in the same factory as Vlado, was elderly. By the end of the week and because he had worked long hours, the brother had little time to prepare messages. Vlado not only had time to prepare the messages, but sometimes had opportunities to go over them with the man. Vlado found it interesting to sit in the congregation on Sunday mornings and listen to his own sermon being preached by someone else!

After he had labored at the factory for only a short time, Vlado arrived at work one morning to learn that his department manager had died. Usually a committee made up of the most faithful Communists in the factory would select a speaker and then have his name approved by the Trade Union. However, on this occasion a fellow worker suggested that Vlado be the speaker.

"We all know he has been a lawyer and knows how to express himself well. I say we get him to speak for us," the man said.

Vlado knew he would be on trial this first time. In fact, one of the factory secretaries came to him with a request.

"Comrade Director fears you will speak too long at the funeral. He requests that you write out your speech and give it to him tomorrow."

Vlado knew the *Comrade Director* feared more the spiritual content than the length of his speech, but he was used to dealing with situations like this over the years. He wrote out a short speech and gave it to the director.

At the funeral, the director of the factory spoke first and talked directly to the dead man.

"Comrade," he said, "we thank you for your labor. You may have died, but your work lives on forever. Your life will continue in the memory of your friends."

It was Vlado's turn to speak. He stood and, with a loud voice, addressed the men in the hall.

"Is the meaning of life only to work, or is labor only to live? Is the meaning of life only to die? When life is so brief, as it has been for this man, do we look forward to life after death? I ask these questions in order that you might seek the answers."

He had made them think all right.

On another occasion, a worker from another department committed suicide. He had been accused of stealing money from a box in which workers put their money when they purchased drinks and snacks. After the police interrogated the man and searched his belongings, he followed several of his friends to a local inn for drinks. Later he excused himself, saying he was going home.

After the man had been absent from work for a few days, officials went to visit him. They found him hanging from a tree in his garden.

No one wanted to speak at this man's funeral. Many of the workers believed he was guilty of theft, yet they had no desire to say so at a funeral. They turned again to Vlado.

"Of course, I will do it," Vlado replied. "But first you must allow me to speak with his family. I did not know him."

"Certainly," agreed the manager. "I will get his address for you and give you a day with pay to take care of this matter."

At least eight hundred people from the large factory attended the funeral. Again, a representative of the Communist Party spoke in a soft voice directly to the body. Few could hear what he said. At the cemetery, Vlado stood on a mound beside the grave and with a loud voice began to speak to the sea of faces before him.

"In the old book Goholet (the Hebrew name for Ecclesiastes), it is written . . . ," Vlado began. He read the first six verses of chapter twelve, ending with "or ever the silver cord be loosed, or the golden bowl be broken, or the pitcher be broken at the fountain, or the wheel broken at the cistern. Then shall the dust return to the earth as it was; and the spirit shall return unto God who gave it."

"In this quotation from the old book," Vlado said, "is a wonderful description of old age and death. Life in these verses is described as a cord, a bowl, a pitcher and a wheel. But the silver chain can snap, the golden lamp can fall and break, the water jar can be shattered. Our bodies will return to the dust of the earth. This is what has happened to our co-worker. Why was his life *broken*? Because, when he needed a friend, no one was there. There seemed to have been no one who really cared, or he would not have been left alone in his trouble."

"The death of this man is a great warning to us that we have a responsibility to love and help one another," he concluded.

Afterwards several of Vlado's co-workers approached him. "Doctor, when I die, will you speak at my funeral? It was an excellent speech."

"An excellent speech?" he exclaimed. "I am depressed because I am not able to speak the real truth that Jesus Christ died for our sins and arose for our justification, and that whosoever believes in Him, though he were dead, yet shall he live."

The Lord gave Vlado other opportunities to speak at private funerals where he had more liberty to "preach unto them Jesus." He became widely known as one who knew how to comfort and give counsel during times of sorrow. Men began to discuss with him their various problems, and their questions about life after death and other matters of faith. When Vlado worked the afternoon shift and the bosses had gone home, the men felt more liberty to speak to him. Often as he swept up at the end of his shift, he could judge the length of the discussions and how many men had talked to him by the cigarette butts around his work area.

Vlado seized every opportunity to witness for Christ. After leaving the factory, he wrote a personal letter to the head of the department in which he had formerly worked, sending him greetings at Christmas and at the New Year. The supervisor later responded:

> Dear Comrade,
> I have just received your kind remembrance and greetings to us all. I passed your letter on to Comrade Vokac so that he can give your greetings to your old co-workers at their next meeting.
> Thank you, personally, for your kind words. Believe me, I often think of you. I am thinking of your good nature, and your interest and enthusiasm for work which could be taken as an example by others. I do not write these words just to flatter you, for I have thought many times that it would be much easier for me to do my job if all of my workers would be like you.
> Please accept from my wife and me best wishes for health and happiness for you and your family. To you, especially, I wish much success in your work.
>
> Sincerely yours,
> G——

Vlado came to realize that his four years in the factory had turned into one of the most productive periods of his ministry. God had given him a work bench for his pulpit and men in working clothes for his congregation.

An early church father once said, "It is up to a man of God to be a witness wherever he goes and, if necessary, to say something!"

15

You no longer have permission to preach
České Budejovice: 1966-71

"Dr. Fajfr will work in this factory for the rest of his life where we can keep an eye on him. He will *never* be permitted to preach again until the day he dies. In addition, he will be constantly assigned to a department in the factory where there are no young men. He has too much influence with them."

The leader of the Communist Party at Vlado's factory responded harshly to requests by church leaders that Vlado be allowed to resume his ministry as a lay preacher. On two occasions they had sought permission for Vlado to work in the factory during the week and preach on the weekends. Each time the requests were denied.

Never is a long time, but it was 1965 and the early winds of *Prague Spring* were beginning to blow. There was a cry from many to *put a human face on Communism*. The Czech representative at the UN in New York wanted Eastern Europe to send a representative pastor to the Church Center in New York as other countries had. To put on a good face to the rest of the world, the government in Prague agreed, and Dr. Jan Urban, pastor of the Brethren Church in Brno, was chosen.

When the request was presented to the elders of the church, they agreed, on the condition that Dr. Vlado Fajfr of Gottwaldov be allowed to serve in Brno as interim pastor.

The government accepted the proposal and sent word to the factory to release Dr. Fajfr from his work for the time that Dr. Urban would be in New York.

In order to travel on the bus or train the miles back and forth between the church in Brno and his family in Gottwaldov, Vlado used a special pass that cost him half the regular price. However, to maintain this pass he had to get it stamped the first of each month by the church state secretary. Vlado had always found the best approach to these officials of the government was to be cordial and direct. Before long he discovered the secretary to be a very intelligent man.

"I see that you enjoy reading. Who are your favorite authors?" Vlado asked.

When the secretary finished listing the authors with which he was most familiar, Vlado exclaimed, "That is interesting. I have enjoyed reading the same authors, especially when I was a student in university. Which books have you read?"

Over a period of time Vlado and the secretary had many interesting and friendly discussions. When it was time for Dr. Urban to return to Czechoslovakia and Vlado to return to the factory, Vlado paid one last visit to the state secretary.

He shook the secretary's hand. "It is time for me to go back to my job at the factory," he said, "and I want to thank you for all your kindness to me. I pray for God's richest blessings on you."

"You won't be going back to the factory," the secretary replied. "Confidentially, I have given a good report of you and your work, and I have recommended that you be allowed to pastor again. I advise you to leave Gottwaldov and go to a place where you are not so well-known."

* * *

"Let's start packing, Jirina, you are to be a pastor's wife again!" Vlado shouted excitedly as he arrived home. Though he did not undervalue his years at the factory, he was thrilled for the opportunity to be back in the pulpit again. The leaders and congregations of his denomination were as happy to have him back as he was to be back. A congregation in Ceske Budejovice, South Bohemia, called Vlado to be their full-time pastor. He was also to have responsibility for five smaller churches, whose lay pastors looked to Vlado for spiritual direction and support. Vlado's car could be seen almost anytime of the day or night along the roads leading to these small churches, such was his joy at being at the task once again.

* * *

One of the most thrilling stories of those years in Ceske Budejovice had to do with a woman whose father was a major in the secret police. Her husband was converted first through very unusual circumstances. In despair because their marriage had failed, he attempted to escape to the West through Yugoslavia. He was caught and imprisoned. He made friends with another prisoner who had been caught in a similar circumstance. After serving their time, the two friends were released and each went his separate way. One day, however, Mr. Navotny decided to visit his friend whom he had met in prison.

After greeting one another, Mr. Navotny offered the other man a cigarette.

"Oh, I'm sorry," he said, refusing it. "I don't smoke anymore."

"I don't believe it!" Mr. Navotny replied. "You used to smoke constantly. How did you quit?"

"I have become a believer, and Jesus Christ has given me

the power to give it up. You know, He could do the same for you."

"I'm not so sure. I've tried to quit many times."

"I'll tell you what. We are having an evangelist from America speak at our church this week. Why don't you stay a few days and go with me to the meetings?"

Curious to meet an American, Mr. Navotny stayed. Upon hearing the gospel later that week, he received Christ as his Lord and Savior. The man was from Ceske Budejovice, so the Christians gave him the address of the church that Vlado was pastoring. Soon he became a regular attender.

After being released from prison, the man had been reconciled to his estranged wife. Now, however, she was upset because he had become a Christian. Her father was a high ranking secret police officer, and she was secretary of the Trade Union Committee in the town. But the Communist Party had denied her membership into the party because of her husband. Still, she was so convinced of the tenets of Marxism that during her free time she visited schools, propagating the Communist regime and its ideology.

One night, nevertheless, she agreed to attend church with her husband. It was Wednesday night Bible study time, and Vlado was calling the people to repentance. He said that they were far from being Christ-like. They needed to have the love of Christ fill their hearts—love for their families, for their neighbors, even love for their enemies.

Mrs. Navotny could hardly believe what she was hearing. The message was nothing like she had expected.

She returned home from the meeting that night, knelt beside her husband, and confessed her sins and unbelief before the Lord. She became a new creation, and the Lord healed her marriage. Soon her mother, her sister and her husband, and her youngest sister all came to know Christ Jesus. Their conversions stirred the saints, and were the beginning of an awakening in the congregation.

Later, in her testimony, Mrs. Navotny testified, "I couldn't help comparing. In our Trade Union meetings, the speeches were so full of pride and hate. Our members could only think of how they could trample on someone else in order to gain more power and prestige.

"In the church was love and caring. I realized these people were right. I was the one who did not know the truth. What did I know of love? Why, I even hated my husband!"

* * *

Times were changing. Dubcek had been chosen as General Secretary of the Communist Party in Czechoslovakia, and the people were elated. He had coined the phrase, *Communism with a new face*, and he believed in a socialistic kind of democracy. Consequently, a whole new way of life opened up for the people—freedom of speech, freedom of press, freedom of religion, freedom to travel abroad. Suddenly, it was as though the entire country were having a party! The years of 1967 and 1968 became known as *The Dubcek Era* and later *Prague Spring*.

To Vlado it meant many new opportunities not previously open to him. His active mind was filled with possibilities for getting the gospel into the hands and hearts of the people. The first thing he did was write several tracts and have them printed. For years this had not been possible under Communism.

Two of the tracts became very popular and were distributed by the thousands throughout the country. One was called *A Recipe for a Happy Marriage*, and the other, *The Book Most Read by the People*. Vlado and the young people of his church went down to the Teachers' Training College and the University for Agriculture in their own town and passed out tracts. Often it led to an opportunity to speak with students about the Lord. They also visited hospitals, and occasionally dared to slip some in the mail boxes of private homes. No stone was left unturned in an effort to get out the gospel while the door was open.

* * *

Another ministry was opened to Vlado while visiting England at the invitation of a dear friend, the Rev. W. Stuart Harris, a former missionary to Czechoslovakia. With this brother, Vlado traveled throughout England, giving his testimony and soliciting prayers for his country. At this time he heard about Trans-World Radio in Monte Carlo, and its ministry of beaming the gospel throughout Europe. In fact, he learned there was a biweekly Christian program broadcast into Czechoslovakia.

Before returning, he took meetings in West Germany, Switzerland, and Austria. While in Vienna, he was contacted by Stuart Harris to use their studios there to record messages for their Czech broadcast. This he did with great joy. After the Dubcek Era ended and the Russians occupied the country, Vlado and his wife were still granted permission to go to Monte Carlo to record fifty messages on tape. Later, however, it became impossible to send sermon tapes through the mail. Amazingly, a contact from Monte Carlo would appear at the needed time. Usually under cover of darkness the sermon tapes were secreted across the border, only to be later broadcast into Czechoslovakia.

The contact with Stuart Harris was profitable in another way. In the coming years, there was a great shortage of Christian literature, and bringing such material into the country was strictly forbidden. But the European Christian Mission and Mr. Harris did not forget their Christian brother in Czechoslovakia. On the first visit the contact came by only to establish a time and place to be used for the "drop." Then the literature began to flow in. A car would roll to a stop in front of the house in the middle of the night. A couple of large sacks would be carried to the small attic at the top of the house. Then the car and its driver would disappear into the night, leaving its precious cargo behind. The Fajfrs were always excited to discover in the sacks Bibles, tracts, Christian books, and children's literature. Just as quietly and secretly as the literature had come to the Fajfr's house, it was distributed around the churches of North Bohemia.

In 1968, *Prague Spring* erupted into a massive protest against the Communist ideology and Russian influence. Writers held forums and students gathered all across the city to discuss their ideas of freedom. Factory workers met to discuss what kind of demands they should make to their foremen. A breeze of change was in the air. But it was not to be. In a matter of days, Russian tanks entered the city of Prague, and though the hearts of the people were strong, their defense was not. It did not take long for the arm of Russia's influence to be felt even in Ceske Budejovice.

Vlado's activities had not gone unnoticed by the authorities of the town. All during the latter sixties, they held their peace but watched. Now, as their influence once again increased, they made a decision. If they were to show their loyalty and keep their jobs, they must act. In 1971, they sent Vlado word: "You no longer have permission to preach."

Mrs. Navotny, who was now a stalwart in the church, took things into her own hands and went to the authorities. "This is not right. Dr. Fajfr saved my marriage from divorce. He is doing a very profitable work in our town. I demand justice!"

Her efforts were to no avail. In fact, knowing the turn Mrs. Navotny's life had taken through the influence of Vlado Fajfr, the Communist leaders were more determined than ever to silence him.

16

The Lord takes Jirina home
Usti nad Labem: 1971-75

Once Vlado received word that he could no longer pastor the church in Ceske Budejovice, he knew he would have to move his family to make room for the new pastor. Telling his family was difficult. The children were older now. Jana had already left school and had her own special group of friends. Daniel was close behind and preparing to enter college. Mark had just entered his teens.

But he had to break it to them. "You children already know I've lost my permission to preach. A new pastor will have to come and live in this house now. It means we have to move."

"But where will we go?" one child asked.

Vlado and Jirina looked at one another. "We don't know. We are still praying. I'm telling you this so that you can pray with us."

The years in Ceske Budejovice had been happy ones for the Fajfr family. Now they were being told they must pack up and leave. It was hard to pray, "Thy will be done," but Vlado and Jirina earnestly sought the Lord.

Soon they heard of a vacant church apartment in Usti nad Labem in North Bohemia. Vlado felt in his spirit that this was the Lord's hand guiding them. They could live in the apartment in return for caretaking duties, and the little Czech

Brethren Church which met in the same building would give him an opportunity to serve the Lord, even if it were as an ordinary member. Since the apartment was free, it would be possible to live on the small pension he was receiving from the government. The Lord had provided again.

The Fajfr family moved, and, as was his nature, Vlado threw himself into the activities of the church. He visited the sick in their homes and in the hospital, ministered to the shut-ins, and acted as a self-appointed usher. Standing at the church door at the beginning of each service, he greeted everyone with a kind word and hearty handshake. In return, the believers of the assembly wholeheartedly received the Fajfr family. It was a great day for the Fajfrs and the church when God directed them to Usti nad Labem.

Once, while on one of his regular visits to the hospital, Vlado met the district church secretary who at the time was a patient. The two men introduced themselves and began talking. Vlado showed a genuine interest in the secretary's health. Later Vlado visited the secretary a second time.

"Is there anything I can do for you?" Vlado asked.

The secretary was visibly touched. "It is lonely here. My family lives some distance away and I see them very little. I look forward to your visits and our talks."

Vlado visited him often after that. One day as they were sitting in the hospital garden, he approached the secretary about his desire to once again preach.

The church secretary replied, "Yes, I think we can arrange that. But only here in Usti will you be allowed to preach."

* * *

For years Jirina had suffered from severe headaches. After the Fajfrs moved to Usti the headaches increased in frequency.

She went to the doctor and he diagnosed her as having multiple sclerosis.

Month by month, the family anxiously watched her strength ebb away. The children and Vlado took on more and more of her responsibilities as she became bedridden. For any mother this would have been hard, but for Jirina it was almost unbearable. Capable to the extreme, she had been like a rock to the entire family. In the deprivations, loneliness, fears, and dangers that had come with being Vlado's wife, she had met them undauntedly. To be helpless, that was the ultimate trial. Yet, Jirina faced this new hurdle as she had faced them all, with courage and a solid faith in her God.

Now it was Vlado who stayed home. Friends and family were amazed to see a new side of Vlado whom they had always known as the tough sportsman type. Gently, he cared for his wife, trying to make her as comfortable as possible. The children found their father almost as good at *mothering* as he had been at *fathering*. It was a new experience to have him at home when they came in from work or school. In this time of tragedy, the Lord began to bind the family closer together than it had ever been before.

After four years of suffering, the Lord took Jirina to her heavenly home in 1974. An autopsy revealed that she had an advanced brain tumor and that she must have suffered more than anyone ever realized.

In later years, as her children reflected on the past, they wished their mother could have seen her dream come true. Often she had told them about the dream in which she had seen Vlado's son—and hers—standing before her in the pulpit, preaching with the power of God upon him.

Jirina had a lifelong desire to see her three children serving the Lord. Only by faith did she see it happen. Did she know that each of her two sons would say he was the one she saw in the pulpit? It could be. Yet, it is not her dream, but her prayers that the children credit for all three being active in the Lord's work.

17

You are the Lord's choice for me!
Usti nad Labem: 1975

When he was single, Vlado always convinced himself that was the best kind of life. After he married, he changed his mind and became convinced that married life was the best. Now that Jirina had gone to be with the Lord, he discovered that it would be difficult to find another wife who would seek "first the kingdom of God and His righteousness." They were few and far between.

Vlado needed someone who would be a right hand to him as he pastored and evangelized. Furthermore he needed someone who would be willing to open their home to everyone, as his first wife had done. It was a tall order, but more and more he realized the difficulties in pastoring among women, especially among widows, as long as he was alone.

A year had passed since the death of Jirina when Vlado received an announcement that his dear friend and mentor, Dr. James Stewart, had been called home to be with the Lord. James had married an American missionary, Ruth Mahan, who at the time was the director of a Women's Training School in Budapest, Hungary. In 1939, a year after their marriage, James and Ruth visited Brno to hold meetings in Vlado's home church. James preached, Ruth taught, and the people were blessed. But that was 36 years ago, a very long time since Vlado had seen James and Ruth.

Vlado remembered Ruth only faintly, but he realized that as James Stewart's wife, she would have all the qualifications he was looking for in a wife. He began to pray for Ruth that, if it could be the Lord's will, she and he would be brought together.

Once while Vlado was reading Psalm 2, the first words of verse eight jumped out of the page: "Ask of me, and I will give you. . . ." Without reading any further, he bowed his head and prayed, "Oh, Lord, give me Ruth Stewart to be my wife. You said, 'Ask of Me, and I will give. . . .' I am asking you." From that moment on he had assurance that God had heard his prayer and would keep His promise.

In 1975, Vlado received three invitations to go to the West to preach. One invitation was from a friend, Wolfgang Heiner, founder and director of Missionsgrupe, Frohe Botkschaft (Joyful Message) in West Germany. The second was from W. Stuart Harris, president of the European Christian Mission, who asked him to go to London for meetings. The third was from a friend in Derby, England.

At the time, it hardly seemed possible that he would be allowed to accept the invitations. But he decided to try. He applied to the Passport Office for the required passport and at the State Bank to obtain dollars since travelers were forbidden to take Czech crowns out of the country. At first his requests were denied. Trying a second time, however, he received permission to travel in both Germany and England.

"It is a miracle!" the man at the State Bank told him. "I can't believe that they have granted you, a pastor, permission when hardly anyone else is allowed to travel." Vlado could have told him that he had given the authorities so much trouble, they probably were hoping he would leave and never come back!

But he saw an even greater miracle. Corresponding with

Ruth Stewart, Vlado discovered that she planned to visit her son, Jim, who lived in a town not far from London. And she was to be there at exactly the same time as Vlado! This had to be the Lord's doing. Vlado tried to hold back his excitement as he made arrangements to meet Ruth.

When they finally met, he knew assuredly, "This woman will be my wife!"

During their two-day visit, Vlado and Ruth talked about a lot of things. Ruth was interested in all that had happened in the past 36 years in Czechoslovakia, especially since she was gathering material to write a biography of her late husband. Vlado told her of James's visit to Brno and of the blessed, lasting results of his evangelistic campaigns. He spoke of many converts from other towns who were remaining faithful to the Lord during the difficult times under the Communist regime.

As the hour drew nearer for Vlado to catch his train back to London, he wondered how he would approach the topic uppermost on his mind. He decided to be as direct as possible. That had always been his method, and most of the time it worked.

"Have you thought about marrying a second time?" he asked.

Hesitating for a moment because she was not quite sure how to answer, Ruth replied, "I can see how you as a pastor really need a wife, but as for me I haven't—"

"You don't understand. I am asking if you will marry me," Vlado interrupted. He began to explain how the Lord had dealt with him.

"I am convinced you are the Lord's choice for me," he said with conviction.

Later Ruth confided to him that she had been so taken aback by his proposal that she had hardly known what to say.

They had really known each other for only two days, and here he was wanting her to marry him and move behind the Iron Curtain? Still, being the kind of woman she was, she gave the Lord the benefit of the doubt.

"I will do anything the Lord tells me to do, but, you see that I must first pray about it." Still shaken, she could at least say that much.

Vlado suggested that they should write each other regularly and that after some time—perhaps a year or two—the Lord would reveal to her what He had revealed to him, that she was to be his wife.

"I shall write you the first of each month," he proposed, "and you answer on the fifteenth of each month." With this agreement and a handshake, they said good-bye, she to return to the States with her head in a whirl and he to Czechoslovakia with a great deal of hope.

The correspondence began. Before long the letters increased in number and length, and Vlado and Ruth completely forgot their original plan. In fact, after only three months he received that special letter for which he had been waiting.

Quoting from the Book of Ruth, Ruth Stewart wrote, "For whither thou goest, I will go; and where thou lodgest, I will lodge; thy people shall be my people and thy God my God. Where thou diest, will I die, and there will I be buried."

The letter arrived a few days before Christmas. Vlado couldn't have received a better Christmas present!

When he shared the wonderful news with his family, they were not so sure. "Will you go to the United States to live?" his daughter asked.

"Of course, not." Vlado replied. "Ruth has agreed to come live with us here in Usti."

"What?" Jana answered quickly. "This Ruth wants to live with you in a Communist country? I wonder! . . . "

18

To all the nations
Abroad: 1976

But Ruth did go to Usti, much to the amazement of her friends on both sides of the Atlantic. She took with her a God-given love for Vlado and his country, and an American passport. The one thing Vlado needed besides a wife was the passport. That would fulfill a promise the Lord had given him thirty years earlier.

One day in 1942, Vlado had been under a heavy burden for revival. He determined to fast and pray. Not one to do things halfheartedly, he decided to go seven days without a bite of food or a drop of water. Though he learned better later on, he fasted with an honest desire to humble himself before the Lord. The last day of his fast he went alone into a park where there was a small forest. There he sat down on a bench with his Bible. "Lord, speak to me through Your Word!" he cried. "Reveal to me Your plans and purposes for my life."

With this prayer on his lips, and a great longing in his heart, he opened his Bible and began to read. He immediately realized that he was reading Paul's testimony to young Timothy as recorded in II Timothy 4:17.

> Notwithstanding, the Lord stood with me and strengthened me, that by me the preaching might be fully known, and that all the Gentiles might hear; and I was delivered out of the mouth of the lion.

In his Czech Bible, the words "all the Gentiles" read "all the nations."

"What a wonderful assurance of protection for me as I proclaim the Word in these difficult days," he thought. "But what a strange promise is this, 'that all the nations might hear!' Here I am shut up under the Nazis with no possibility to leave the country under any circumstances. What then can He mean?"

Puzzled, but sure that the Lord had spoken directly to him, he hid these words in his heart.

Thirty or more years passed, during which time he had occasion to remember God's assurance of protection and strength in difficult times, and he often shouted, ". . . and I was delivered out of the mouth of the lion." However, the borders of the country were still closed. The Nazis left but the Communists took over. Foreign travel became almost impossible. Still, Vlado held on in faith to God's promise that he would one day preach "to all the nations."

That is where Ruth's American passport came in. Because the Communist governments of Eastern Europe were still advertising to the West the propaganda that their people had great freedom, how could the Czech government deny an American's request for her husband to accompany her to America—*or Mexico, or Singapore*? So it was that during the first ten years of their marriage, Vlado was able to travel with his wife to many lands—from the United States to Canada and Alaska, from Mexico and the Bahamas to Great Britain and Scandinavia, from Japan and Singapore to North and South India. Perhaps the greatest miracle of all for Vlado was the permission the Communist government gave him to spend some time in the state of Israel. In each of the countries the Fajfrs visited, Ruth had friends among the missionaries who opened doors for Vlado to preach the gospel. Indeed, the Lord fulfilled His promise to allow Vlado to preach "to all the nations."

During his many visits to foreign lands, Vlado never lost his vision for his own country. He had an even greater burden to see God work mightily. In His providence God had placed Vlado in Czechoslovakia and to that country he always returned with an increased expectancy of what the Lord was going to do.

19

The wind bloweth where it listeth
Usti nad Labem: 1971-83

Usti nad Labem was the largest city in North Bohemia and its commercial hub. The church in this city was considered the "mother church" to many smaller churches in the towns and villages surrounding Usti. Only one full-time pastor was allowed for the entire area though other men qualified as lay-pastors. Understandably, Vlado was thrilled in 1973 when he once again received permission to preach, even though the permission was limited to the church in Usti.

The church languished. The congregation consisted mostly of elderly women and widows. Apart from the Fajfrs, only a couple of other young people attended the services. At first, there was very little change. Vlado visited the sick and elderly, made contact with family members who did not attend church, and in general cared for the needs of the church as best he could. On Tuesdays he led the juniors in their special meeting and on Friday nights, the young people's meeting which five or six attended. There was not much to encourage him.

Then came Vlado's marriage to Ruth. The Lord seemed to pour new life and vision into him. By this time, Vlado's son Daniel had graduated from the university and was working in the computer department of a nearby factory. He had recently answered the call to preach and was preparing himself for ordination through a correspondence course. Meanwhile, he took over the work with the young people.

Often around the dinner table, conversation among the Fajfrs would turn to the days of the great revival that flourished in their country just before World War II. As in many Christian homes, photos would be brought out and stories told and re-told. In reflecting over those days, it seemed to the Fajfrs that the Lord in His providence had been preparing His church to go through the fire and deep waters of which Isaiah spoke in chapter forty-three.

"But that was forty years ago," one of the children would comment. "Look at things now."

"I know," Vlado would reply. "I wasn't saved at that time, but I still remember how it was. What we must not forget is that the revival came in answer to prayer. Everyone was praying. Morning, night, anytime of the day they were free, they would meet to pray."

"Do you really think God could do it again?" someone asked.

"Why don't we start meeting every morning before work?" Daniel suggested. "I know my friend will want to meet with us."

Vlado, Ruth, and Daniel and his friend began to meet early every morning in earnest, united prayer before the Lord. After the two young men left for work, Vlado and Ruth continued, mentioning one person after another whose names were on a list laid before them. Their prayers were definite and concrete.

Before long the Lord began to answer the prayers. Unsaved husbands began to attend church with their believing wives and children.

In one instance, the Lord used the serious illness of a wife to speak to a husband's heart. The man phoned Daniel one evening and said, "At last I am on my knees before God."

He and his wife became an example of the grace of God and a delight to the whole church. The wife, though paralyzed on one side, became one of the prayer-warriors behind all the Lord was doing in their midst. Her glowing face spoke to everyone of the reality of her love for the Lord.

Members of the church who had been *ordinary church members* now were being blessed by the Spirit in unusual ways. A young mother was saved during an evangelistic effort and she brought her children into the church meetings. Soon the men were meeting together to pray. Then a few of the women asked Ruth if she would meet with them for Bible study and prayer. Though a small beginning, it was the prelude to a work of the Spirit that would far surpass their most believing prayers.

The Lord's work among the young people was especially thrilling. One young girl in the youth group, Jana, was a sweet Christian but quiet and rather shy. The Lord began dealing with her heart, and finally in one service, she gathered enough courage to speak up.

"Those of you who know me will know how difficult it is for me to speak. In my high school, I am the only Christian. Please pray for me that I will be a witness," she timidly asked.

That was all she said.

But the Lord heard her prayers and the prayers of others on her behalf. She faithfully carried her Bible with her to school and in her own quiet way left an impression on those around her. One of Jana's classmates was full of life and fun. As Jana was quiet, this girl was noisy—a real *enfant terrible*. She began to question Jana about why she carried her Bible and about the youth meetings she attended.

"Why are you not in the Young Communists Band?" she asked. The questions opened a door for Jana to tell the classmate about Jesus Christ and the gift of salvation that could completely change her life. To everyone's utter astonishment, Zuzanna joyfully embraced the gospel.

And keep quiet about it, she couldn't! She told everyone. The entire school was abuzz with the news. In fact, during the class usually devoted to teaching Marxist ideology, students began to ask questions about God, the Bible, and salvation. Class periods turned into lively discussions between the two girls and their classmates.

At the end of one class, a student jokingly wrote on the board that the SSM (the Communist Youth Organization) would meet, and he gave the address of the church and the date of the next youth meeting! When that day arrived, five boys from the class showed up to mock and disrupt the meeting. They left sobered and impressed.

"What is so bad about this?" one boy whispered to another.

Four or five classmates were saved through the witness of Jana and Zuzanna. The first was a friend of Zusanna's, Hana. She attended the youth meetings with Zusanna, heard the singing and testimonies, and saw the look of peace and joy on the faces of the Christians. At the end of the service, she turned to Zuzanna and said with tears in her eyes, "Now there are three of us who believe!"

Many others, who were confronted with the gospel for the first time in their lives, later received Christ Jesus as their Lord and Savior. One of the newly converted young ladies was the daughter of a military colonel. At first, she kept her newfound faith a secret, but after her baptism she knew she had to tell her father.

"What? Do you realize that I have only two years before retirement? Now, I will be dismissed in disgrace. How could you do such a thing to me?" her father shouted. Nevertheless, the young lady continued to meet with her fellow Christians.

One young man who attended the youth meetings was the son of a KGB officer. Many, like him, attended the services secretly, but soon found they could not keep it to themselves. Persecution followed. High school officials were not happy with the *bad influence* these Christians were having on the student-body. Parents were called in and reprimanded. They were told that if their daughters did not keep quiet, they would be dismissed.

Often in the youth meetings the young people made tearful requests. "Please pray for me. My parents have forbidden me to come. They think I am at my ballet class, but I can't stay away from the youth meeting," one young girl said.

"I need wisdom to know what to do," another added. "My parents are upset with me because they want me to go to the university. Now that I am a Christian, it is obvious I won't be allowed to go. I wanted to be a teacher, but it's not possible now. Perhaps I can find work on the railroad."

"I won't be here next week. My parents told me if I continued to come, I would have to leave home. I have nowhere to go," exclaimed one.

Despite persecution of the young people, they attended the meetings in greater numbers. To hear their testimonies and their singing was proof enough that God was doing a great work in their midst. Day and night young people concerned about their souls were visiting the Fajfr house or the church for counseling. Both Vlado and Daniel found it a full-time job pastoring the flock. Vlado was in his element as he moved from place to place in line with whatever the Holy Spirit was doing.

Ruth was right in the flow, mostly praying. She likened the work of the Spirit to a forest fire.

"Just when the devil thinks he has put it out in one place,

it breaks out in another," she said. "It reminds one of the verse in John 3 that says, 'the wind bloweth where it listeth,' and none knows 'whence it cometh or whither it goeth.'"

20

It might be good for me to leave Usti
Usti nad Labem: 1983

With people being saved and young Christians needing to be discipled, Vlado and Daniel found that there were hardly enough hours in each day even with their combined efforts. Still, it was a glorious work. The church had truly been revived. Each Sunday the church building was packed, filled with their faithful regulars, the new believers, and many seeking visitors.

As always happens, however, the Devil was also at work trying to undermine the genuine advances in the Kingdom of God. Nevertheless the leaders knew how to combat their enemy. They went back to the place of prayer, back to doing business with God, and back to resisting the Wicked One. As 1980 passed into 1981 and 1982, it became clear that what the Lord had done was a lasting work with everlasting repercussions.

Then the hammer fell. All at once one of the sisters in the church was summoned to appear before the secret police. They questioned her about what was going on in the church. Later the same day, the lady's husband was called in from work and asked virtually the same questions. When this continued throughout the week with other members also being "brought down to headquarters," fear began to grip the congregation.

As he expected, Daniel was called in by the authorities.

From the questions asked him, he concluded that someone had been reporting on the church's activities.

Vlado was ready. He knew the kind of questions the police would ask, and he had prepared his answers. For days, he waited and prayed. Instead of sending for Vlado, however, the authorities sent for the young pastor responsible for all the churches of their denomination in North Bohemia. He in turn went to Vlado with the bad news. Permission for the Fajfrs to preach had been rescinded.

Surprisingly, not many pastors in Czechoslovakia lost their permission to preach. When they did, however, there were usually two reasons behind it. One was for speaking against the Communist government, the other for winning young people to the Lord.

Strangely, the church in Usti had now lost *both* pastors in one day. Vlado had few problems with not speaking openly against the Communist government. But leading young people to the Lord came so naturally to him, there was nothing he could do about it. They seemed to be drawn to him and he to them. The second and third time Vlado lost permission to preach was because of his success with young people.

"We must be careful, but not afraid," had always been his motto. During the years of Communist control, many pastors were fearful and used so much precaution that their ministries became ineffective. Vlado believed implicitly that his times were in God's hands, and nothing and no one could touch him without His Father's permission.

When friends warned him to be more careful, he would shrug his shoulders. "Why worry?" he would say. "It's no problem with God."

Now Vlado had an opportunity to prove God one more time. As he had found out before, there were so many ways to serve the Lord without having to actually preach. And if anything, the Fajfr men were enterprising. Often on Sunday and Wednesday evenings, the church members would form a circle with chairs around the hall and have a "discussion" about a certain portion of Scripture. Many joined in, and who was there to object if Vlado's or Daniel's remarks were a little lengthier than others? There was no pulpit, so who could be accused of preaching?

Daniel also saw this time as an opportunity to strengthen the growing youth group. Because of their lively singing and enthusiastic testimonies, they soon received requests from all over Czechoslovakia to minister. At the end of each program, Daniel took the opportunity to give a short evangelistic *talk*. Many were saved and encouraged in their faith. At the same time, the youth group from Usti and nearby Teplice found themselves maturing spiritually.

Still it was difficult. Sermons that could not be denied burned in Vlado's heart. Nothing could take the place of preaching. One day as Vlado was waiting in prayer, a thought came to him which he felt was surely from the Lord. The next day he visited the district church secretary's office.

"I have been thinking," he told the secretary, "that it might be good for me to leave Usti and find a position somewhere else. Do you think if I leave, perhaps Daniel might get permission to preach again?"

The man was thoughtful. To be rid of Vlado Fajfr—that was certainly something to consider. This preacher had been trouble from the first. He couldn't be controlled like so many others.

"Yes, I think it is altogether possible," the secretary said, barely suppressing a smile on his face.

21

Foreigners are invading our fair city
Zilina, Slovakia: 1983-95

Zilina is a beautiful old town in Slovakia surrounded by snowcapped mountains. Its 100,000 inhabitants are primarily Roman Catholic; in fact, the town has a history of strong Jesuit influence. The university in Zilina has a student-body of approximately five thousand students who come from all parts of Slovakia and the Czech Republic to prepare themselves for jobs in transportation and communication.

To most people, however, Zilina is the gateway to the Fatra and Tatra Mountains, Slovakia's *playground* during both the winter and summer months. In just an hour one can be in the mountains, skiing, climbing, or enjoying the spectacular scenery. Because of this, the streets of Zilina are often filled with tourists and students, as well as local residents.

It was to this town, just an hour away from Mt. Chleb, that the Lord directed the Fajfrs. Here two young couples were in the process of planting a church while carrying on a ministry with the university students. Already several young people had been converted, but someone of Vlado's experience was needed to establish the work.

He was thrilled! Vlado's mother had been Slovak, and often as a child he had spent long periods of time with his grandparents in this beautiful country. As children do, he quickly picked up the Slovak language and cultural traits so that it became his second home. Now, years later, he was well-known in all parts of the country through his years of service in the churches. Besides, he loved Slovakia. Often folk accused him of being more Slovak than Czech. It took little to convince Vlado that this was the Lord's place for him.

But one did not just *move* in a Communist country. Certain permissions had to be sought. Then there was the problem of a place to live. Thousands were on a waiting list for an apartment.

Believing the Lord was directing them, Vlado and Ruth made a trip to Zilina, willing to accept whatever the Lord provided. Much to their astonishment, instead of a small apartment, they were able to purchase a large semi-detached house that had just gone on the market.

As they walked through the house, Ruth was thrilled with the large, sun-filled kitchen and began planning how she would arrange it. Vlado paced out the size of the living room, visualizing it packed with people, listening to the gospel. The bedroom was almost as large and could double as a study. Upstairs were a large bedroom and a bath that would be perfect for the visitors who were sure to come.

Without much ado, the Fajfrs were able to purchase the house. With the generous help of Christian brothers, they made a few alterations to the home and moved into it in July, 1983. From the beginning there was a stream of visitors passing through. On Monday it might be a pastor on his way home from a special meeting, and on Tuesday, a family on their way to a few days of vacation in the Tatras. On Wednesdays, students often dropped in to speak English with Ruth and share their testimonies of how they came to the Lord. Thursday through Sunday, missionaries from Germany, or the Bahamas, or Copenhagen might arrive for a time of fellowship, prayer and refreshment. It meant shopping, cooking meals, and making beds while setting apart time to be sensitive to the spiritual needs of each person who landed on the Fajfr doorsteps.

Adding this to the task of building a fledgling group of believers into that unit called a *church*, Vlado and Ruth faced the facts. They had certainly not come to Zilina to retire! But who wanted to slow down now? More and more university students were attending the Bible Hour. Many heard the gospel for the first time and with hungry hearts trusted Christ. There were so many to be nurtured and guided through the rough waters of spiritual *infancy*. In a real sense, these young people became the Fajfr's children in the Lord, and, just as in a natural sense, this brought joy and triumph along with heartbreak and disappointment.

The Fajfrs prayed for families with young children to be brought into the church. The students came and went after four years. What the church needed was a nucleus of long-term members. The years passed; the prayers persisted. Slowly at first, and then more regularly, the Lord brought in the young couples Jozko and Katka, Michal and Alyna, John and Zlata, Brano and Ema, Dusan and Marcela, Ivan and Rachel, and finally the new pastor, Dusan Jaura with his wife, Zora. And with these couples there came children.

With success in the gospel ministry, there is always opposition. As the numbers outgrew the small meeting place, the church met together to plan how they could expand. First there was the problem of the deed which was still in the name of one of the couples who purchased it in the first place as a residence, not as a church. Then a problem arose with a neighbor who insisted that any renovation to the building would throw a shadow on her house. In her petition to the city council, however, she made clear the true reason for her actions.

"These foreigners (Czechs) are invading our fair city with a sect (anyone not Roman Catholic) that is suspicious," she said, "and one can feel some behind-the-scenes moves of a well-premeditated influence on the local population!"

For a while, it appeared this woman would have her way, even though the coming of the Velvet Revolution wiped away all other hindrances. Oh, how the prayers of the saints bombarded Heaven. The Lord answered. Today you will find a beautifully renovated meeting place that is testimony to God's power!

Now in their eighties, there were times Vlado and Ruth longed for rest and quiet. Wasn't that the reward of old age? But, the Lord wasn't finished with them. There was one more message to preach, one more burdened heart to soothe, another sister or mother or daughter to visit and to tell the story of God's grace, just one more time. Obviously, the only retirement they were to enjoy would be the Lord's return or their homegoing. What a glorious anticipation!

> We have great
> expectations as heirs,
> not of fading earthly
> things, but of God's life
> in us forever.
> —Author Unknown

Epilogue
Zilina, Slovakia: 1995

We live here very well. It is a happy life I have with such a wife as Doris Ruth Stewart Fajfr. She now has eighty-six years, and I, eighty-five. Today, we just came from a walk. Oh, it was wonderfully fresh. I must tell you that now I have so many years, my wife doesn't allow me to go swimming in the lake in November as has been my habit for so many years. She also makes me wear a hat and boots when it is raining. Can you believe how she babies me? But it's a small thing to please her. Still in the winter, I can do a little skiing, and in the summer, I often go to the river to swim. The movement is good for me.

Many people congratulate me on my years. But I am not guilty that I was born; my parents are the culprits and they are dead. But it is great grace that I am alive until now and have such health. Without grace I would be a long time in the grave—not only in the grave, but in hell! Every day I praise the Lord for His grace to me.

But you must know how it is with us now. From the time of the Velvet Revolution on November 17, 1989, we have had freedom in our country. I prayed for this for years—to be able to preach the gospel freely—and did not think to see it in my lifetime, but here we are. After years of problems, we have been able to enlarge the meeting place for the church.

But, you ask, what can two old people do? God gives strength. Once a month at least, I preach at the church and my dear wife gives an "Introduction to Prayers." Often I am busy writing an article for our denomination magazine, or devotional book. Often neighbors will come to speak English with my wife, and she is able to talk to them about the Lord. Others come for the fellowship or to discuss problems.

Best of all is Monday nights when our neighbors are coming to us for a little meeting in our living room. Many years I speak to them on the street. Now they come. To all it is new. They never have heard the gospel before. Now they are listening and join in the singing, and even ask for prayer. I am believing God to save five people from our street. So many prayers He has answered in my life. Why not this one?

My children? That is also good news. Daniel is one of the leaders among the Czech Brethren churches. He is still pastoring in Usti. You know, under Communism, we were never allowed to build. Now, if you would go to Usti, you would see the largest new church building in North Bohemia! Such a joy it is to us to see what started fifteen years ago, still going on. Jana, my eldest, has stood faithfully beside her brother in his ministry and is a valued servant in the church.

Mark? He is now also a pastor in Teplice. What vision he has! In a short time he has opened up two new branches, and labors day and night to reach villages untouched until now with the gospel.

I think everyone's life has a message. The Apostle Paul said, "Ye are our epistles, known and read of all men." I pray that reading this story of events in my life, you will see one thing—"God is faithful." At all times. In all situations. This eternal life which we have been given, not only will it get us to Heaven, but it will stand up under all conditions—sickness, poverty, attacks, troubles, persecutions, and even under the difficulties of Communism.

> For the life was manifested, and we have seen it, and bear witness, and show unto you eternal life, which was with the Father, and was manifested unto us.

—Vlado Fajfr
1995